Miracle Man

Patrick McNeese

ISBN 978-1-0980-7745-7 (paperback)
ISBN 978-1-0980-7746-4 (digital)

Christian Faith Publishing, Inc.
832 Park Avenue
Meadville, PA 16335
www.christianfaithpublishing.com

Printed in the United States of America

CONTENTS

PREFACE

*W*ebster defines miracle as "an extraordinary event manifesting divine intervention in human affairs."

This book is dedicated to the miracle of my life, my wife, Ivy McNeese. When I was forty-six, I had decided that I better become comfortable being single; and when I did feel okay being single, I met my wife.

You will find that this book is defined mostly by the physical challenges I have had and continue to have throughout my life. I was told many years ago by Jim Willard, my mentor and second dad, "Pat, we do not have problems in life. We have challenges." And I have tried to think that way for many years. He also said I have not had a bad day since I have been sober. I may have some bad moments, but I can change my day anytime since a day is only twenty-four hours. He proved to be true to his word when his son Greg, an NBA referee, passed away due to pancreatic cancer; and he still said, "I have not had a bad day, but I sure have had some very tough moments." You will find in reading this book how many people have influenced my life, but not have influenced more than Jim Willard; and I thank God that he came into my life and helped turn my life around, from a complaining immature adult into a responsible man who takes responsibility for his actions.

ACKNOWLEDGMENTS

I would especially like to thank my daughters, Delcito and Little Ivy, who have no idea how much I love them and how they have influenced my life to be a better man, husband, parent, and granddad.

There is BB, Bible Boy, or some people know him as Francisco, whose dream is to become a Christian minister and is already touching many lives.

A special thanks to my grandson Jayden, better known as Watermelon Boy, for being the son I never had and showing me how awesome he is and how intelligent he is with the added burden of having autism. I have to say that Jayden has taught me more than I could ever teach him because of his disability with autism.

I would like to thank Gracie, my granddaughter, who finally liked me when she saw how crazy I was one time eating out at a Mexican restaurant, when she was two years old.

I want to thank everyone in my family including my elder sister Jane and her husband, Darryl, for always taking care of me in times when I needed their help. I would like to thank my elder brother Bob, who has always been my hero, from the first day I remember to his coming back from the Iraq War and hearing how he commanded his squadron, the Wild Weasels, being the first to assault and destroy the enemy's weapon arsenal and how his back seater told us that he was the greatest fighter pilot he had ever known. And he mentioned due to my brother's great flying skills, he saved their lives several times from antimissile attacks.

Mike has a special place in my heart, because he introduced me to an AA that was not a glum lot but showed me being sober meant having fun and enjoying life to the fullest.

Chris, the youngest of the five of us, showed me courage and strength when I saw firsthand how he handled being critically ill as a young child and/or baby.

And to end, a special thank you to a special and dear friend, Daisy Vu, who really inspired me and motivated me the past three months during the coronavirus pandemic to finish this book.

That proves to me that even though we as a whole in the United States may find seemingly unbearable burdens put on us, there is always something good that can come out of it.

This book is about me, Patrick Francis McNeese, and the challenges and miracles that have taken place in my life over the past sixty-seven years. I have been told by numerous friends that I should write an autobiography, and so that is what this book is about. To be honest, I started this book in 2001 and got stuck on a chapter I named "Procrastination"!

Now, eighteen years later, I have renamed it and started it over because of the circumstances that have recently occurred in my life. It is my hope that whether you are a Christian like me or you don't even believe in a god, after reading this book, you will laugh, cry, and ultimately realize that yes, miracles do happen in this hectic and chaotic world we live in.

I want to stress that much of the beginning of this book is composed of stories that my mom told me when I got older. I want to make this point very clear before you begin to read this book, because I want you to know that my challenges in life don't come close to the severity of the challenges that so many individuals face. I cannot even imagine how they have gotten through them with dignity, self-respect, and courage. I could never imagine myself being able to handle and get through them.

1

Brief History of My Parents

My dad, Francis "Frank" McNeese, was born on March 21, 1915; and he passed away in 2008 at the age of ninety-two, which all but the last year were healthy years. His last year was spent in a convalescent home because he was suffering from dementia. He was one of five siblings. He had two elder brothers, an elder sister, and a younger brother. They were raised in Los Angeles, California, and they were raised mostly by their grandmother as devout Catholics. Their mother died when my dad was around eleven; and therefore, the reason they were raised by their grandma was when their mom passed, their dad was not home that much because he was out of state most of the time, helping construct high electrical wires. His two elder brothers, along with my dad, were good athletes. They went to a high school that was in the hills, just a mile or so from what is now Chavez Ravine (Dodger Stadium). The eldest in the family, Allen, became a professional boxer; and Tom, the second eldest brother, was a great football player, where he started as a running back at Gonzaga University, which at the time had one of the best college football programs in the nation, and he went on to play professional football. My dad was a starting quarterback in high school and would go on to start at a local junior college. I'm not sure if his younger brother Barney played any sports while in high school.

Growing up, we were closest to my dad's sister, my aunt Ronnie, who was my godmother; and from the time I was young up until she passed, she would give me a $20 bill for Christmas. We never knew or saw Allen, but every so often, Tom would show up out of the blue. From what I was told, Allen turned into a heroin addict, while Barney was an alcoholic. One summer, Barney painted our house, and I helped him. I really liked Barney, and one reason was he would always encourage me when he saw me play baseball. One time, he was very drunk, and my dad was out of town, and my mom called my dad to see what she should do. My dad told her to call the police, and I heard her call them. I didn't want him to go to jail, so I took him, and we walked on the beach so they wouldn't find him. I thought maybe that would sober him up, but no, he eventually got arrested. When he went on a binge, he would wind up on Skid Row in Los Angeles; and a few times I went with my dad, trying to find him so my dad could take him to a place to try to get sober. I always thought my uncle was special, and that might have been because as you will find out, I too would be an alcoholic. Barney could never seem to sober up, and his wife told me she believed it was because he could never be honest with himself.

My mom's mom and my grandfather were recovering alcoholics and more than a few times had Barney stay with them to try to get him to sober up, but he would always wind up going back out and getting drunk. I remember one story my grandma said that my uncle would look for anything with alcohol in it, so they would even hide everything that might have alcohol. One time he went into the barn, and he found horse limonite and drank it. My grandparents couldn't believe that it didn't kill him. He finally had gotten around five years sober, when I had a little less and was doing good. Then my aunt called me and told me his roommate had called and said Barney had gotten drunk. So I drove to Redondo Beach to check on him. His roommate answered the door and said he was passed out on the bed and had gotten pretty beat up. So I went in his room. He was passed out, and the whole side of his face was full of bruises and cuts. I couldn't believe how beat up his face was. He was to the point that nothing would wake him up, so I left and told my aunt there was nothing I could do that day, because he was passed out. I told her I would go back and check on him in a day or two. A few nights later, I got a call from my aunt saying he was in the emergency room of a hospital, and she asked me if I would check on him. She called me around eleven at night, so I said I would go by the hospital first thing the next morning. Barney got discharged that night and somehow got on one of the freeways and was hit by several cars. I always thought, *What if I had gone to the hospital that night!* But I decided, and people told me, not to second-guess myself. Hell, he might have already been discharged, even if I drove up to Los Angeles to check on him.

My dad's dad, from what my mom said, was a very gentle and loving man; and my mom really loved him. I don't remember that much, but she said he would take me for walks and really like it. He was staying with us on Lido, and one night he had bad chest pains, so my parents called an ambulance. My mom said that when they put him in the ambulance, he waved goodbye to her, letting her know that would be the last goodbye. And it was because he died either on the way to the hospital or at the hospital. My dad had a wake for him at our house, and all my dad's siblings showed up, even Allen whom my dad had not seen for many years. I think it was the first time my mom had met him. But it was nice that all my dad's family got together to mourn the loss of their father.

Ruth Frances Wright McNeese

My mom was born on March 19, 1928, and passed away in 2011 of lung disease. She was one of two children. She had a younger brother, Bob. Mom's whole family traveled out to Long Beach, California, from New York. She was born in Long Beach, along with her brother. Mom's dad died from emphysema when she was around fourteen. He was in an emphysema ward the last months of his life, and she couldn't visit for fear of catching it. He passed away during World War II, and not long after that, my grandma joined the army, and my mom and her brother moved in with her grandparents in Iowa. She would eventually live in a Masonic lodge. At that time, it was where kids would live if they had nowhere else to live. My mom said she actually didn't mind living there. I believe my grandmother started to drink heavily after her dad died, and she would find AA and get sober around 1947. She met my grandfather through AA.

2

Early Years

I was born on June 21, 1952 (the beginning of summer and the longest day of the year!), in Long Beach, California. I was born into a family that already had two children: my elder sister Jane, approximately four years older, and my brother Bob, one and a half years older than me. When I came out of the womb, I knew something was wrong. My mother took me home with my dad, and there were these little people waiting for me. How could I be in a family where I was not the special one?

From early on, my life was full of physical challenges. That seemed to be a major portion of my life experiences. When I was approximately nine months old, I came down with the German measles. This is not a big deal, except that my dad who was an officer in the United States Navy was being transferred to the Pentagon in Virginia, and my parents did not want to travel with a sick baby, so for the next six to nine months, I lived with my grandparents. By the time I flew to Virginia with an aunt and arrived at my home, I had no clue who my mom and dad were, let alone these two little people who appeared to be taking too much time from my mom and dad. What the heck. How come I was not the only child in the family where I could be spoiled rotten? I think I probably was spoiled, especially since my parents had not seen me for at least nine months.

My earliest misfortunes started shortly after I arrived in Virginia. I was riding in the front seat with my dad in his car, and he had to stop suddenly, and my head went crashing into the windshield.

I was taken to an emergency room, and my mom said she had a harder time trying to calm down my dad than look after me! Thank God I was not hurt seriously. I believe I just needed a few stitches.

The next incident happened when I was around two years old. I guess I had some kind of virus, with a bad cough. In those days, they didn't have vaporizers, but my mom had a pot with boiling water that caused steam to get into my lungs. She wrapped me up in bed, so I couldn't get out of bed, and I fell asleep. I guess I woke up, managed to get out of bed, and stepped right into the boiling water. My mom said she had to take off my feet pajamas, and I guess a lot of skin was taken off also. They rushed me to the hospital, and I had second- and third-degree burns from the bottom of my feet up to my knees. The recovery was long enough that I had to learn how to walk again! That is when my sister and brother gave me my first nickname, Paddy Waddles; and from then on, I knew I was different from my sister and brother. How could you not be different with a name like Paddy Waddles?

We eventually moved back to California. I think I was probably three or four, and I believe we moved back to Long Beach. When I was around five, we moved into a model home in Costa Mesa, and after only being there a short time, my mom got pregnant and had my younger brother Mike. Since the house was too small for three children, we moved to Lido Isle, in Newport Beach, and lived there until I was nineteen or twenty. I went to a Catholic school the first part of first grade, and then my parents transferred my elder brother and me to Newport Elementary, a school whose playground was the beach! I guess the nuns said I was probably not real smart, because I was not learning as I should be learning. I do not at all blame the Catholic church because I'm sure a lot of it was my perception and may not have taken place as I try to remember. All of us kids were raised Catholic; and my brother Bob and I went to a Catholic school up until first and second grade, while my sister went to a Catholic school most of her life, even going to a private girls' high school, until she transferred to a public high school her junior year.

3

Elementary through Junior High School

My dad had been an amateur boxer, maybe even a Golden Glove boxer; and almost before we could walk, he had me and Bob boxing each other, and I mean hitting each other. This would last probably until we were at least ten or eleven. He was always tough, and if he was training us and we hit him too hard, he would come back and hit us as hard as he could. We had a speed bag that my brother had put in the garage, and we were constantly hitting it. I actually got pretty good at being able to hit it. I really did enjoy boxing, although my brother Bob was much stronger and could see better, so I was mostly getting hit, instead of doing the hitting. Getting hit never really bothered me; it would get me pumped up.

I remember that I was told that God made some kids smart and some kids just average, and then we don't know why, but sometimes God makes kids dumb and clumsy like me.

One time when I was in the confessional booth, I asked the priest why everyone in my family seemed to be coordinated, athletic, and smart; and I was the opposite, uncoordinated, clumsy, and not real smart. He said we don't always know God's reasons, but everyone is made unique. I even remember Bob and I were altar boys, and Bob always served with the priest and another altar boy, helping with communion and such, and I was like an extra who sat on a bench and watched them serve mass. I couldn't even be a real altar boy.

I had a great first-grade teacher at Newport Elementary who told my parents, "I don't think there is any problem with Patrick's learning ability. I don't think he can see." So I was taken to an eye doctor who found that I not only couldn't see but was legally blind. The good news was that he felt my eyes hadn't fully developed, so for the next year, I spent more time having therapy on my eyes than I did in school. Due to this fact, I was set back and started first grade over, instead of advancing to the second grade—another reason I felt different then. But the miracle was that after all the therapy, my eyes were 20/20, although the doctor told my parents not to hold their hopes up for too long because they could deteriorate again. But what I remember was incredible, because the first thing I noticed was that from a distance, people had facial features, a nose, mouth, and ears. The second big thing I realized was that trees actually had leaves; they weren't just some big glob of green.

I believe around this time in my life, I received my second nickname from my brother and sister, which was Gutter Boy, because when it rained, I liked to walk in the gutter! Another reason I was different from my siblings.

I also had a speech problem where I didn't pronounce my words correctly, so I had go to a special class where they worked on my pronunciation. I remember even my name bothered me. Looking back, when I was young, I wish I went by Patrick, instead of Pat. I always felt less than because my name was Pat, and some girls had the same name, so it really bothered me a lot, especially in elementary and junior high school.

In addition, both my sister and my brother were gifted with being athletic, while I was clumsy and always falling down or hurting myself. It seemed to me that they were much smarter and talented than me in all areas of life. At least that is how I remember myself being. I especially wanted to be like my elder brother, because from early on, he was my hero and very coordinated, as was my sister.

I said I had the nickname of Paddy Waddles; but as we all got older, everyone in the family would have nicknames, including my mom and dad. My dad's was Potbelly; my mom's was Ruthie; Jane's was Janey Lizzxy Snazzy Pooo… whoo-hoo, that's you. I gave Bob his because one day he had on a pair of shorts, and there was some kind of dirt spots on his butt, so I called him BM (Bob McNeese) Spots. That didn't go over too well, so I can't remember if he beat the hell out of me the first time I called him BM Spots or later on. When I was mad at him, maybe for teasing me and to get back at him, I would always call him BM Spots. Chris's nickname was Big Head, because he was so small and skinny it looked like he had the head the size of an elephant!

Mike actually got his nickname from my dad, because when he didn't do good on a test or a report card, my dad would say, "You're nothing but a rum dumb..." This was when he was probably fifteen or sixteen. And to this day, if you call him Rum Dumb, he will look at you and say, "Those are fighting words," which would happen if we were both drunk and I called him Rum Dumb.

One time when my parents were out of town, we had a party, mostly with just some close friends; and I got so drunk I passed out in bed. Well, they were making a bunch of noise; so I came to and starting arguing with Mike about what a shithead Dad was, never complimenting Mike on anything, especially football. It pissed me off because he did that to Bob and me, and I didn't like him doing it to Mike. Well, somehow the word *rum dumb* came up in the conversation, and he hit me so hard in the nose that it broke, but there was so much blood, it had looked like Charles Manson had paid a visit to our house. Yes, I had a broken nose and also another concussion!

Although I seemed to always be the tough kid in elementary school, I'm sure most of the kids probably thought I was a nerd, because I did some nerdy things, like being a safety officer, which meant I directed traffic at recess and lunchtime. I think nowadays I would definitely have been considered a nerd. I always seemed to attract positive attention through fighting and was always the tough kid in elementary and junior high school. I remember in high school a kid whom I went to elementary and junior high with was an offensive and defensive tackle, so he was a big kid even in elementary school. One day in high school, he told me he was actually scared of me in elementary school, because I didn't care how big a kid was (most were bigger than me). I would still fight them, or they would not want to fight me.

From the time I was young, I was addicted to candy or anything with sugar. It got so bad that my mom would try to hide any candy we had. It got to the point where she hid it in her underwear. Guess what? I found it. I could never just eat one piece. If I had an opportunity, I would eat the whole package in one sitting. If my mom gave me money to buy lunch, and I rode my bike to school, I would not eat lunch but go to a local small grocery store near my elementary school and spend it all on candy. Now remember, back then candy bars were only five cents, so I could get a lot of candy with fifty cents.

My brother and I were involved in Cub Scouts and Boy Scouts, and my mom was always a den mom, and my dad was somewhat active in Boy Scouts. Bob was always the lead guy, and needless to say, I followed him. By the time we were twelve or thirteen, I think both of us were mainly still in Boy Scouts because of the campouts. Also, they had what I think was called a jamboree. I will never forget one time when everyone was asleep, we got up and took the pegs out of the tents all over, so they collapsed. I think we actually did the headquarters tent also. My brother eventually left, and I stayed in for maybe one more year.

The scoutmaster was a guy we called Tag, and he also was active with the kids on Lido in the summertime. We used to joke around and talk behind his back, because I believe he lived with a sister, and I think there was something wrong with her, so he was like a caregiver. I was pretty burned out with the whole Boy Scout trip, so in the fall when the first meeting took place and new kids were joining, I was a troublemaker. At the end of the meeting, we did the scout oath; but I had my own oath, which was something along the lines of "A scout is an idiot, a scout is a pussy, a scout is a momma's boy," and on and on. The only problem was that unbeknownst to me, Tag was standing behind me and heard all this. I guess he heard enough to the point that he took the thick scout book, hit me on the side of the head, and said, "Get out of here and never come back." Since it was the first meeting, all the parents were there, although I don't think my dad was, because I don't remember getting in trouble.

As I mentioned, I got bloody noses very easy and many times had to go to the hospital to get my nose cauterized. I think the doctors said my capillaries were on the service of my nose.

It never bothered me when something happened to me to cause me to bleed, but if I saw someone else in my family in pain or bleeding, it freaked me out. I remember one time my brother Mike was riding his bike when he was ten or eleven and took a shortcut from the sidewalk into some ivy. There was a sprinkler head that he hit, and he was barefoot, so he came riding into the garage, with his toe barely hanging on his foot and bleeding badly. I remember yelling, "Mom, Dad, Mike's toe is off!" and they came running in the garage. I think I then fainted, and one of them had to take care of me while the other one took care of my brother. He had incredible pain tolerance, unlike me; and at the time, he was the quarterback for his Pop Warner team. A week later, he was playing in a playoff game, with his toe still all stitched up.

Another time while he was in high school, he was returning a kickoff and straight-armed a guy, but one of his index fingers got caught between two helmets that took off the end of his finger. I went down to the sidelines to see what happened, and his finger and hand were all wrapped up, and so I asked, "What happened?"

He said, "Look!" He took the goddamn tourniquet and bandages off, then out his finger came spurting up blood a foot high. Did I pass out? I don't think so, but I know I got sicker than a dog. Maybe from the blood and maybe from too much beer. Mike was very coordinated and athletic, and he also was always the leader of all his friends from elementary school, all the way through high school. My elder brother would always protect him, so if he bugged me, Bob would be behind him and say something like "What are you going to do about it?" Well, one time my brothers didn't see my dad behind them, and he saw firsthand what was going on, so he told Bob to get the hell away from Mike. Then he said basically, "Pat, beat the shit out of Mike."

Well, Mike was maybe eleven, and I was probably sixteen; not a fair match. I really didn't want to hurt him, so I hit him with the back of my hand. Guess what happened? You guessed it, I broke my hand. I will never forget my mom saying something like "It is only Pat who would not want to hurt his brother, and in doing so, he hurt himself." I had a cast on, I think, for six weeks and didn't play much baseball that summer. In fact, when the doctor was sawing off the cast, the blade got caught in the wrapping under the plaster and twisted my wrist around. My mom screamed at the doctor, "You just broke my son's wrist!" He took x-rays, and yes, my wrist was broken, and he told my mom it must have been broken when I first broke my hand and the x-ray didn't catch it. I think my mom was so mad she said, "You are full of shit," but needless to say, I had another cast put on for four to six more weeks. Luckily people didn't sue doctors back then.

When I got older and would bleed, something in my head would get triggered; and if it was caused by someone else, like a fight, I would literally want to not beat the person up but hurt them baldly to the point that if I had a weapon, I think I would have killed them. I think in a way it was lucky I drank so much, because most times I was so drunk I could not beat myself up, let alone anyone else; so it helped me from really going off the deep end. My father was a fighter pilot during World War II and the Korean Wars, and by the time my brother and I were seven and eight, we both wanted to be fighter pilots. We had a closet full of toys, and we used to put small chairs in this toy closet and pretend we were astronauts or fighter pilots.

By the time I was eleven years old, my eyes had deteriorated; and without glasses, I once again was legally blind. I will never forget when my eye doctor had a heart-to-heart talk with my mom and me and let me know that my dream of being a fighter pilot would never happen because of my vision. I remember this really affected me; once again, I felt I was not good enough. My brother would live his dream and make a career in the United States Air Force as a fighter pilot.

As I mentioned, my siblings at the time were much more coordinated than I, and this was proven when we would go to my grandparents' home in Huntington Beach. My grandparents had approximately ten acres of land, less than three miles from the Pacific Ocean, and had horses; and my grandfather would grow wheat and corn and other vegetables. My brother and I had a pony named Buttons, and my sister actually was an excellent rider and trained one of the colts that was born to one of the horses. My brother took off on the pony like he had ridden for years. Me, I was scared to death of this huge animal, and Buttons knew it. My grandmother told me, "Don't let the horse know you are scared!" Easier said than done. That pony took off for the lowest tree and knocked me for a loop. I can't remember if I fell off or not; but my granny, being the five-foot dynamo that she was, put me back on the saddle until I no longer was scared to ride.

I loved riding on my grandpa's tractor on the weekends when he would plow the fields to grow wheat. It was one of the funniest times I remember between the ages of six and eleven. In addition, I used to help weed where the corn grew with my favorite hoe. It had two prongs on the end, so it was good for me to use. When the corn and other fruits and vegetables would ripen, my grandparents would set up a stand on the street off Golden West in Huntington Beach, and we would sell to local Huntington Beach residents. I loved spending the weekends with my grandparents because my grandpa and I were very close, and I would always ride on his tractor while he plowed or planted crops. I loved spending time with him, and I can remember that they got the first color TV in our family, and we all went over and watched a popular TV show on a Friday night.

The last few years of my grandmother's life, she was not that well and spent a lot of time in bed. I remember she had gotten hit or somehow injured her brain, and they were trying to get her strength up to be able to operate. One time when she was in the hospital, we were visiting, and I don't think kids could go in the room, so I was outside, maybe with Bob in the cafeteria area, and there was this lady there with her arm and hand all wrapped up. We asked her what happened, and she said she cut her fingers off with a saw. The next thing we knew, she brought out a bottle and said, "Look, here are my fingers." Well, as young kids, my brother probably thought it was funny; but I think I almost passed out. I know my mom wasn't too happy when she found out, and we left that area pretty quickly.

The summer I was in the seventh grade, going into the eighth grade, Bob and I went to a sports camp for two weeks at Santa Clara University. It was a lot of fun, and we slept in the dorms as if we were students. The coaches were great and really nice. I had a great time until the last week. I will never forget one night I had a dream, and all I remember was my grandma keeping on saying, "Don't worry, Paddy, everything is okay. Don't worry, Grandma is okay." Well, that morning, my parents had called the coaches and told them my grandma had passed away and that they knew I would really be upset, along with Bob. So I think they called us in one at a time or maybe together and told us. I was really, really upset. They told us that our mom had told them that Grandma would really want us to stay the remaining time at camp and not to go to the funeral. So we stayed and didn't go to my grandma's funeral. I remember shortly after we got home, my mom took us or me to the cemetery and showed us where she was buried. I remember thinking to myself, *Watch where you walk. You don't want to walk on a dead person!*

My grandparents had slept in separate bedrooms for years, and I guess the last few years, my mom suspected that my grandpa was maybe seeing someone. Well, a week or two from coming back from camp, I would spend the weekend with my grandpa, and that would be the last time I would spend with him. I guess he was seeing someone and also contested the will, saying my grandma wasn't in her right mind when she drew it up; and so instead of my mom getting like five acres, she would get two or two and a half acres. She wasn't so mad about not getting the property; she didn't give a crap about that. It was that he had the nerve to say that her mom was not in her right mind.

I remember a few years later riding my bike to the house from Lido and peeking in the window and seeing kids in the house with a lady. I will never forget it. I rode off crying like a baby, thinking, *Why did my mom not allow me to see my grandpa? I love him, and now he has other grandkids.* Wow, I was really upset because I had so much fun spending time with him and sleeping in the same room with him. Another time, I remember my grandma telling my mom, "For god's sake, I don't sleep with Chuck. I think he only takes a shower once a week!"

At that time in the early and late '50s and early '60s, Huntington Beach mostly consisted of bean fields and oil well derricks. One of the exciting things my elder brother Bob and I got to watch was them tearing down an old wood oil well derrick that was on my grandparents' land.

Know when I was about five, I let Bob use my favorite hoe. Now remember I was legally blind, and no one knew it. My brother swung the hoe, and not being aware that I was directly behind him, one prong went into the corner of my eye and ripped part of my nose off, according to my mom. They rushed me to an emergency room, where they stitched me up, and thank God I guess it barely missed ripping my eye out.

When I was eleven and twelve, I had some experiences that I will never forget. The first one was when I was eleven. One evening, I was home with my dad and my brother and sister, while my mom had gone to a play in Hollywood with a good friend. My dad, who loved boxing, was listening on the radio to a fight; and as I remember, both of us were lying in the living room, when suddenly I started having the worst stomachache I'd ever experienced and started throwing up uncontrollably. There was a doctor and friend who lived near us, and I believe my dad had my sister or brother run over and get him to come to our house. Doctors actually made house calls back in the day. He came over and immediately told my dad I was having an appendicitis, and I'm not sure if I went to the hospital in an ambulance or if my dad took me, but that night, they took me into surgery and removed my appendix. I can't remember if my mom got to the hospital before I went into surgery, but I remember my dad being so scared that I actually saw him cry for the first time, since his dad passed away when I was five or six. I remember waking up the next day, and my dad had got me the most expensive baseball glove a kid could have. It seemed to make all the pain go away. My dad, as you will find out, was very emotional when one of his children was hurt.

From the time I was four or five up until I was sixteen or seventeen, my nose would bleed to the point that my parents would have to take me to the emergency room to get it cauterized; they could never get it to stop on their own.

One of the saddest days in my life occurred on New Year's Eve when I was eleven or twelve. One of my best friends whom I would see almost every Sunday at the Catholic church we went to had been trying rope tricks, tying a rope to a chin-up bar that went between a doorway. I remember hearing that his parents told him never to put anything around his neck, because it was dangerous. My dad knew that I was very upset and wanted me to talk to a priest and also talk to his parents to help me deal with my grief. Even though I was a Catholic, I could not understand how God could let my best friend die. I never did talk to the priest or his parents. A few years ago, over fifty years since he had passed away, I got a hold of one of his sisters and let her know that for all this time I had wanted to let someone in his family know how much I grieved for her brother. She was so understanding; and when I hung up, I was crying because after all these years, I finally had talked to a family member. I don't believe it was coincidence that early on a December 31, the day Kenny passed away, I went to his grave site, not being there for over fifty years. This might seem incredible, but after all those years, it was like God directed me right to his grave marker, and I put flowers on the site.

From early on, elementary school through high school, I never thought I was good looking, so I never had any girlfriends in junior high or high school. Looking back when I was thirteen or fourteen, as a boy, you pray to God to give you hair in certain areas. Well, as everyone knows, God has a sense of humor and made me look like a gorilla when I took my shirt off. No one in my family that I am aware of has a hairy back. I know for a fact my sister or mom doesn't. Ha-ha. Now that I am older, he really has a sense of humor, because it's growing on top of my nose, in my nose, on my ears, and in my ears. My god, if I didn't trim or have someone take care of all my hair, they would say that they finally found the Sasquatch man; and he wasn't in the forest after all these searching and reported sightings. I actually lived in the city…ha-ha, and that is also worth a BA for all my friends I grew up with in high school.

When I was a senior in high school, the Newport Beach Police Department got a helicopter that we named the Whirly Pig, and people actually would use pellet guns to shoot at it because people were beginning to think it was Big Tom, short of ironic with what is going on right now with the coronavirus.

When I was around five, my parents moved from Lakewood to Costa Mesa, California, in a new tract home development; and we moved into a three-bedroom home. We had great neighbors, and I remember I always thought the family next to us was great, because their dad was a marine. We really didn't live there that long because my mom got pregnant with Mike, and we needed more room. I remember at least one Fourth of July, and it was a lot of fun. It was also the first time I went to a football game with my dad; and we went to the local junior college, Orange Coast College, and watched them play. The biggest event that happened while we lived there was the people across the street had maybe a two- or three-year-old who had run out into the street and got run over by a car. My mom said there were actual tire marks on the little body. But somehow, a miracle, the little baby survived.

I think by this time, my dad was making good money; and he bought a home in Newport Beach, on a little island called Lido Isle. We moved there in 1958 or 1959, and our house was in the middle of the island on a street, to a *strada* interior lot. New to us, a strada was a sidewalk. All the streets were named after streets in Italy. Back then, it was made up of a lot of beach cottages, and a lot of people lived there part time, like in the summers and during vacations. When I was little, it had a lot of vacant lots, and so we had fun making forts and underground forts, where we would dig a hole and put wood over it and then cover it with sand. We also would make Christmas tree forts, gathering all the Christmas trees we could that were out for the trash, and make forts out of the trees. It was such a great place to be raised, and I had so many good friends that I grew up with.

I remember when we first moved there, a guy, for some reason, had it in for Bob. He was a few years older and called my brother Taco, because I guess he had a hat on that said taco. When we were young, he would always give my brother a hard time. One time my sister, whom you didn't mess with (she was a teenager), had enough; and as I remember, she beat the hell out of the guy, while one of her girlfriends watched in case she needed help. Well, he didn't give my brother any more trouble. We became the McNeeses early on, because we would not take crap from anyone.

My dad had set up a boxing area in the garage, with a speed bag, and we were constantly working on the speed bag. The frame was made of a sheet of cut-out plywood Bob made; and if you missed the bag, you were likely to cut up your hands pretty good, hitting the wood.

The island had more expensive water front homes that fronted the water with many having docks, and these homes were much more valuable than the homes in the interior of the island. One of the awesome features of the island was that every so often, there was a public beach with a dock, so we had a beach right off the street we lived on and would swim and skin-dive off that beach. It also had a private yacht club, the Lido Isle Yacht Club, where there was a club-house and dock along with a snack shop during the summer.

The first boat my parents bought us was called a sabot, and it was the sailboat that beginners would learn to sail in. During the summer, there would be races against the other yacht clubs that were located within the Newport bay; so at a very young age, we all learned to sail. My sister seemed to be the best sailor in our family and was also a great swimmer. I remember my first race. I think I came in last, ha-ha, because you had to tack the sabots back and forth a lot, and that is why you learned to sail in them. I wasn't great at tacking, so needless to say, I didn't race much. But one of our neighbors was a great sailor, and they used to have what was called the flight of the snowbirds (snowbird was a type of sailboat). One summer, I got to crew for her; and we won the whole regatta, which consisted of many races. I will never forget because it was the first trophy I ever won.

We used to have so much fun, even in the winter, because my brother and I would make wooden rafts; and when even the bay was rough, we would launch the raft and basically go wherever the current took us. There was also a vacant island named Shark Island, and we would always sail over to it and have great fun playing on the vacant island. During the summer, we would play water tag, and my brother and I would seem to always win. We would go underwater and come up underneath a dock, and other kids didn't know how to do it. There was one kid, Tat, whom we sort of thought of as the kid you sort of tease, and he would always be it. My brother and I even said we were Superman and say we could stay underwater for as long as we could and would go under a dock and stay there then swim up to the surface and say, "Wow, Tat, can you believe how long we stayed underwater, without scuba gear?" We also would dress up with caps and make him believe (I doubt he believed). We would say we were going to fly up on a roof; and we would go to the side of a house, climb up the roof, and come to the other side and say, "See, Tat, we can fly."

One summer we were playing water tag, and of course Tat was it, and we would wear fins, so you had to be careful because the docks were slippery. Tat started running on the dock after my brother and slipped and fell. He fell headfirst into the water, while his testicles were hung up on a boat cleat. Thank God my brother was a great swimmer and grabbed Tat and got him on the dock before he drowned. His mom always thought my brother was a hero because he saved Tat from drowning. The sad part was six months or a year later, Tat got testicular cancer and died when he was only eleven. I will never forget because he had gotten a train set for Christmas, so his mom had us come over to play with it while he watched. I don't know why, but for some reason, their bedroom gave me the creeps, and I remember walking home and telling my brother that it seemed like a big coffin. It was only a few days later that the poor kid passed away.

The different blocks would always come up with players to play football or baseball, and the McNeese team would always win. I remember the best sport for me was baseball, and I was a great pitcher up till around seventh or eighth grade, because I threw sidearm, and nobody at that age could hit a sidearm pitcher.

One of the challenges my elder brother had was that when we got old enough, he jumped off the bridge that led to Lido. So my best friend jumped off. Next it was my turn, and I think it took me over fifteen minutes to decide to jump. Another challenge was to go under the bridge and go from one end to the other, sometimes almost hanging on whatever you could grab. Well, I didn't like heights that well, so I never passed that challenge. When we got a little older, another challenge was to climb to the top of an oil well derrick. Well, one weekend my brother and a friend rode their bikes to Huntington Beach and climbed to the top. When they got back and told me, I said, "I can do that."

So my brother said, "Okay, next weekend the three of us will go, and you can climb to the top of one." So the next weekend we rode our bikes to Huntington Beach. They picked an oil derrick that was on the side of a steep cliff, so it even looked taller than it was. I tried to get out of climbing by saying, "I don't believe you guys actually climbed to the top. I might be stupid, but I'm not dumb!"

So they said, "Okay, we will go first, and you follow us."

So I said, "No problem. I will follow you." Well, the derrick was at certain intervals short of a resting place at the ladder, which itself was not very wide. So they got past the first platform, and then I started climbing. I got to the first platform and looked down over the cliff and panicked. It took them at least forty-five minutes to get me to climb down to the bottom so they could get down themselves. That was the last time I ever tried climbing to the top of an oil well derrick. On our way home, we decided to stop at a grocery store near our house and grab something to eat. I don't know if we didn't have any money or if we just decided to steal, but they stole some candy, and I stole an ice cream sandwich. Well, we got outside, and our friend's bike had a flat tire. By the time we were trying to figure out how to make our getaway, the store manager grabbed us and took us to a private room while he called our parents. When he finished calling, he looked at our friend and said, "Man, your dad is very, very unhappy."

I remember asking the manager, "Well, we already are going to have to pay for what we got, so is it okay if I just finish my ice cream? Otherwise, it's going to melt and be a waste of food." He didn't say anything about our dad. Well, when Bill's dad came, he got him; and they left. Being good Catholic boys, you can imagine what my dad had in store for us. He looked at us with his "evil eye." (All he had to do when we were in trouble was give us a look, which we called the evil eye, and we knew we were in big trouble.)

He said, "Okay, get on your bikes, and we will discuss this when we get home." Well, discussing and getting hit with a belt were two of the same things.

One summer, maybe because we were getting older, it seemed like Bob and I were always getting in trouble. Well, my dad had heard of a dad on the island who spanked his son every Saturday, because he knew that he had done something wrong during the week. So when my dad heard about this method, he said, "Okay, every Saturday morning, we will begin the day by me spanking you with the belt." So the next Saturday, he had us in his bedroom with our pants at our knees, and I was shaking like a leaf. He got his belt and said, "Okay, lean over." Well, we leaned over, and he took his belt and barely struck us, so the belt went limp. He said, "Okay, I'm done for this week." Then we stood up, and I believe I had said something like "I have never heard of something so crazy as to spank your kids because you know they did something wrong during the week. Well, hell, if I was his son, I would get in as much trouble as I could, because I was going to get spanked anyhow." Wow, looking back at this, I'm sure glad my dad was compassionate compared to some dads.

When I was in seventh grade, my first report card I flunked every class, including PE. The physical education coach said he wanted to get my parents' attention, and he did!

I remember that same night, I went in to kiss my dad on the cheek while he was lying down on his bed (I did this every night); and before I could kiss him, he hit me in the stomach so hard that I could not breathe. Then he sat up and said, "If I ever see a report card like that again, you will be going to a private all-boys Catholic school." Well, I did good enough in seventh and eighth grade that I did not go to a private school.

The vice principal of my junior high school had gone to school with one of my dad's brothers, so he was always nice to me. I got to know him very well, because it seemed like I spent more time in his office reading short stories regarding sports than I did in the classroom. I was always sent to him for disturbing or disrupting a class. Needless to say, I was the class clown in all my classes. One example is that in eighth grade, I had a teacher who had big boobs. Well, I sent a note to a friend that said, "Wow, this teacher has the biggest boobs I have ever seen."

While passing the note, she got a hold of it, read it, and turned red. Then she looked at me and said, "Patrick, get up from your seat and go directly to the vice principal. Another time she would not let me go to a tract meet because I had not finished an assignment. I got up, and she blocked the door. So I proceeded to the windows and climbed out. Well, I didn't go to the tract meet, but I did visit the vice principal.

There were so many great stories and memories while we lived on Lido. When my mom got pregnant again with Chris, we needed a bigger house again, so my dad bought a house that was on a lot and a half (very large lot for Lido) and had the home remodeled and added on. I always liked to help the workers, so I had a great time while they were adding on. The great thing was it had a big yard and a maids' quarters that was attached to the two-car garage. So the first thing we did was put in a pole so we could play tetherball. My god, we would have battles playing tetherball even when we were in high school. Even my soon-to-be brother-in-law would get in the action. We always thought of my brother-in-law more as an elder brother, because he would always engage in whatever we were into.

At one time, we loved playing tag in homes that were being built, and we would always wind up climbing up and down the frames of new homes being built playing tag! The house we lived in first on Lido was a two-story, which has some significance, because I believe when my sister was around fifteen or sixteen, sometimes she would sneak out of the house by climbing on a little ledge over the garage and having a friend catch her. Well, back then, my dad drank a lot when he and my mom would go out, and he was a mean drunk. One night he came home and found out how my sister was sneaking out, so he wanted to find out how she got back in. So drunk as a skunk, he tried climbing up the front gate. But when he got himself standing on the gate, it came loose, and he fell right on his back. He had a bad back anyway, but he was laid up for days, and I remember we would actually have to help him to get into his Volkswagen bug because his back was so messed up.

I guess when my grandma found out my mom was pregnant with Chris, she was really upset, because I guess they were supposed to use the rhythm method to prevent getting pregnant. My mom had no intention of getting pregnant with Mike, let alone with Chris. So I will never forget my mom telling me that her mom said, "Well, I guess the rhythmic system isn't working, so get your goddamn husband to stick it out the window, before he makes you pregnant again." Ha-ha. Also, my mom got pregnant even after having Chris…

Well, she was in no condition, physically or emotionally, to have another kid. I guess abortions were illegal back then, so she had a friend drive her to some quack doctor in Los Angeles to perform the abortion. Well, I guess she almost bled to death on the way home, and she was in Hoag Hospital recovering. I didn't find this out until my sister told me years later. No wonder my sister believes abortions should be legal. We almost lost our mom, after having five kids, because at the time it was illegal.

I always tried to protect the kids who were being bullied. I remember one time, I was playing basketball with a friend with the hoop at his garage door. We were playing, and for some reason, I guess I got mad at my friend and pushed him. Bob was driving by and stopped and told the kid to hit me. I was not expecting this shy kid to hit me, but he hit me and then ran into his house. I was more pissed off at my brother than I was at my friend who hit me.

My dad never ever wanted anyone to lose, especially in a fight. One time I was fighting a kid and was getting the better of him, and we were on the ground where I pinned him. I said, "Do you give up?" and he said no, so we both got up and started fighting again. This time we got on the ground except he pinned me and said, "Do you give up?" I said yes, and the fight was over. My dad was watching (I didn't know he was watching), and he followed me into the garage. He grabbed me and said, "If I ever see you give up on a fight again, I will beat the shit out of you myself."

Another time, we got off the bus, and a few friends said a kid had been talking bad about me and I should fight him. This kid was a mellow kid, with not a mean bone in his body and had never been in a fight. Well, I beat the kid up to impress my friends. But deep inside I felt so bad. I knew he didn't say anything bad about me. But mostly because I liked him and knew he was not a fighter. From first grade all the way up to sixth grade, most of the same kids would go to the same bus stop. I ran into one of the girls who was my age about twenty years ago, and she reminded me that even when I was in third grade, I was a little crazy, because I would always take her lunch box, but I would give it back to her. She was probably bigger than me and could have beat me up, but even back then, I had a big mouth. Even if I couldn't back it up, everyone thought I could.

With regard to our home life, I really started to get angry at my dad when he treated my mom bad, especially when it came time to pay the bills. I remember him acting like he was much smarter because he had graduated from University of Southern California and my mom had a high school education. He would always call her dumb and taunt her that she did not know how to add and subtract. I remember sitting on the stairs crying because I hated it when my dad treated my mom badly. I remember one time I was sitting on the stairs upset and getting a bloody nose. Well, I went downstairs, and they stopped arguing because they had to take me to the ER to get my nose cauterized.

My youngest brother, Chris, was born; and I was twelve when he came out of my mom. When he was around three, my mom took him to the doctor to let him know that he didn't seem to be urinating enough. I guess the doctor said, "Don't worry, some kids are like that." Not too long after that, they took him to the ER, and they found his urine was being blocked because he had a deformed penis. No, not really, it was the urethra that runs through the penis. So he wasn't getting all the urine out of his bladder. This also caused his bladder and kidneys to not function properly. They hospitalized him, and the pediatric urinary doctor told my parents it looked like his one kidney was so damaged that they were going to have to remove it. It so happened that my mom's uncle was the head of the urology department at Stanford University, so she called him.

Immediately he said, "Do not let them do anything until I see all the x-rays and reports." I will never forget because it was the first time I saw my dad crying like a baby and trying to smoke one of my mom's cigarettes, while he was talking to my mom's uncle on the phone. My dad would fly up to the Bay Area with all the reports and give them to my uncle. My uncle would wind up calling all the leading pediatric urinary doctors in the United States and found a top doctor who worked out of Children's Hospital in Los Angeles. He would spend a lot of time in and out of the hospital to repair his damaged areas. I remember my mom would stay at the hospital most of the time he was there, so a lot of times I would drive me and my dad up to the hospital to see him. I think my dad was so tired from work that I would do the driving

My mom said that my sister was always Daddy's girl, but when she started to get older, he started to treat her badly, and my mom didn't seem to know why. None of us could be good enough, but even the more with my sister. He forced her to go to Catholic schools and my dad did not seem to like the fact that my sister was sixteen years old and like most sixteen-year-old girls was interested in boys. I really felt sorry for my sister because of how he treated her. It made me really angry at my dad that much more. It was bad enough how he treated my mom, but to treat my sister like she was no good really upset me. I remember one time she was sitting on Darryl's lap in our family room, and he came in and threw her through a sliding glass door. None of us could believe it, especially Darryl. It is very lucky that Darryl didn't beat the hell out of my dad. My sister was a natural athlete and a great swimmer, along with being excellent with horses. When she was like fourteen, fifteen, and sixteen, I think my mom had her spend as much time at my grandma's as possible, because that way my dad couldn't treat her badly. I always looked up to my sister, and when she got to be fifteen and sixteen, I thought she was a fox! No wonder boys liked her. We were so glad when she met Darryl and started dating him. One of her boyfriends I thought was a jerk. He would drive up in his car and God forbid if we touched it, let alone hit it with a football.

When we were growing up, there were a lot of different families who would move on our block and not stay that long. I remember they built a new two-story home, and my mom called it the white elephant. I think because it had no character. One of the people who lived in it had a daughter who was a great swimmer and actually made the Olympic team and I believe held the women's world record for the butterfly. I just remember she didn't place in the finals, and everyone was disappointed because at the time, she held the world record. I really felt bad for her when she came home. Her mom, if I remember correctly, just pushed her to no end, and her dad was very mellow, and it seemed like the mom wore the pants in the family. There was also a family that lived near us for while that had two boys who were the tallest kids on Lido, and they both played basketball for Newport Harbor High School. The eldest was a little strange, but the youngest was a really nice guy, as I remember.

My dad on a lot of Sundays after going to mass would have some of the neighbor kids come over for breakfast and make pancakes. I think my mom actually made them. My dad loved to go to baseball games, so we would go see the Dodgers play when they first moved to Los Angeles at the Los Angeles Coliseum while Chavez Ravine was being built. After that, we would go see them play at the new stadium. I was so lucky that I got to see some of the all-time greats play, such as Sandy Koufax and Don Drysdale. Speaking about Drysdale, my parents went to las Vegas one time, and I guess they ran into Don Drysdale at one of the casinos. My mom really thought he was handsome, and when he came up to them to shake their hands, I think my mom damn near passed out.

One of the funniest things that my dad did involved John Wayne, the actor. He and his wife moved across the street from us while their house was being constructed in Bay Shores, a private community. Well, we never saw the Duke; but one afternoon, he was in the front yard watering a few plants. My mom called her local friends over so they could watch him from our living room. My dad being my dad said, "What the hell is the big deal?" So my dad put on a baseball cap—the Duke was wearing one—went to our front yard, and started watering. The funny thing is my dad never watered our plants. But he wanted to make sure the ladies knew that he was also famous. Well, the Duke crossed the street and shook my dad's hand and said, "Howdy, partner, my name is John Wayne; but you can call me the Duke."

My dad with his humor said, "Well, Duke, my name is Frank McNeese; but you can call me Mac!" I thought my mom was going to kill him when he came back in. God, we were all cracking up. My dad had such a funny side to him. While I'm thinking about it, my dad was the one who was the devout Catholic; but I always thought my mom, who didn't go to mass, was much more godlike than my dad.

My dad could crack us up though. Sometimes at church, he would be one of the ushers and collect money. The collection basket was on a pole, and sometimes one of his friends would put money in the basket, but my dad would keep holding it in front of him, like telling him, "Give the church more money." We would be cracking up inside, because it would embarrass his friends. I shouldn't portray my dad as a complete ass, because mostly he was okay, except when he would drink too much. It was amazing that he pretty much stopped drinking when they moved to Bakersfield, and it was like Mike and Chris were raised by a different dad than me, Bob, and Jane.

We had all kinds of friends on Lido, and one of my best friends while in elementary school was a kid named Bill who lived on the other side of the strada from us. His mom and my mom where den mothers for Cub Scouts, so we were pretty close and the same age, although since I had to be put back a grade and go through first grade again, he was actually a grade in front of me. We would have all kinds of activities on the strada, with bikes, made-from-scratch scooters. Bill's house was one of the only homes of my friends that had grass in front of the house, not bushes, and so sometimes we would make tents and camp out for the night in his backyard. One time I had to go to the bathroom real bad and didn't want to wake up his parents, so I pooped on the grass. The next morning his dad came out and was a little angry when he said, "Okay, which one of you pooped on the lawn?"

Bill said, "I didn't, Dad," and he looked at me, and I said, "All I know is I heard a real big dog walking by last night. He must have pooped."

His dad, sort of trying not to laugh, said, "Well, that is the first time I have seen a dog poop like a human." The families that lived near us were all good friends, and one of the families I liked the most was the Perrys. There were seven kids, and I was good friends with the second eldest, Cito. He was younger than me, but as kids growing up, we hung out together. He was so funny. He wasn't skinny, but he wasn't fat, and I say this because he would make sandwiches that looked like he had used a whole loaf of bread. His dad was very successful, but he never spoiled his kids. Another one of the kids was Mike's age, Bill; and he and Mike were best friends, along with a friend named Mitch. One of the daughters' name was Monica, and she was the prettiest girl on Lido. It seemed like every boy had a crush on her. She was so pretty, the head football coach even mentioned her during a team meeting.

Another family that lived next to us was the Haddens, and they had three boys. I will never forget when they first moved in. For some reason, Bob got in a fight with all three and beat them all up. Their mom (Mrs. Kravitz, ha-ha) came over and said, "Either your boy is very tough, or my boys are very weak."

My mom said, "It's probably a little of both."

She would turn out to be the Mrs. Kravitz of the neighborhood. "Oh, I'm not going to let my boys see that movie; it is for adults." Or her husband, who seemed to like to drink, would come over to our house for cocktails; and thirty minutes later, she would be yelling in her backyard, "Rob, Rob, it's time to come home!" He would just roll his eyes, gulp the rest of his drink, and head home. He actually was a really nice guy. When they first moved in, Bob said Mr. Hadden couldn't fight his way out of a paper bag! Of the three boys, Joey was the more normal; he had girlfriends and liked to play sports, especially basketball. I think he took after his dad the most.

We also had another neighbor, and we nicknamed his wife Olive Oyl, because she looked like her. The husband would go down and walk on the public pier every evening like clockwork. One time, Joey was on the dock and asked, "Why do you come out here every evening?"

And he said, "I come out here to collect my thoughts." That made us all crack up, because we had never heard someone say they were collecting their thoughts. Another neighbor we had was a rather large woman, and by saying large, I am being nice. Well, Bob went to her house to collect money for the paper, and he saw a big bag of laundry on a chair just inside the door. He almost fell over, because the bag of laundry got up and paid him.

Another thing we would do in the summer was swim across the bay at the exclusive Balboa Bay Club. It was the high-end of all the yacht clubs, and we would swim over to use their facilities, and they had a nice pool. One time there was a big group of adults, all dressed nicely and walking by me, and I was soaked wet from just getting out of the pool. This one man came up to me and shook my hand, and he said, "Son, my name is Barry Goldwater. Are your parents going to vote for me to be the next president?"

I knew my mom and dad loved John F. Kennedy, and so I said, "Well, I don't know, sir, but I will tell them that you would like them to."

One of the great times on Lido was Halloween, because all the neighbors would give out great candy. My mom said it was my favorite holiday when I was young because I was a sugar junkie, to the point I would fill up a bag, go home, and fill another. On top of that, when I was finished eating my candy, I would eat Bob's and Jane's. It was so bad that if my mom bought any sweets from the store, she would hide them in her dresser drawer, but guess what? I would find them. She later told me she knew I was going to be an alcoholic, because I was so addicted to candy.

Needless to say, I also loved Easter, because we would always get chocolate and candy eggs, and guess what? When I finished mine, it was time to get into my brothers' and sister's Easter basket.

Another great time on Lido was the Fourth of July. The whole street would have a block party, and then we would take fireworks down to the public beach and shoot them off. One year, Mr. Perry bought a keg of beer, and Cito and I would sneak cups of beer when no one was around.

One of the other great things we did as kids, actually up until I was a junior or senior in high school, was play sports on our street. We seemed to always play football; it didn't matter if it was winter or summer, and many times it was just three people on a team. One time one of my younger friends, Tommy, who was actually a good athlete as a young kid, caught a pass and, looking to catch the ball, caught it and ran smack-dab into the front of a car that had like a plane on its hood and hit it full on with his chest. It was amazing he didn't get hurt himself.

It seemed like my mom was the local nurse for all the kids in the neighborhood. One time this same kid came running to our front door screaming. My mom opened the door, and he had taken an ice pick, and it had gone straight through his thumb. He was a tough kid, because my mom gently pulled it out, and he seemed okay. Another time his mom got deathly ill, and they were involved with some type of church that didn't believe in doctors and thought praying over them would heal them. Well, I guess her husband was so convinced, so he came over and convinced my mom to go to their house and talk to her. I don't know what my mom said, but the lady would go to the hospital, and my mom probably saved her life.

Bob would make us scooters out of two-by-fours and put roller skate wheels on the bottom. He would make some with boxes in the front and then also cut out coffee cans and nail them on the front and stick candles in them so we could ride at night. Well, back then, if you farted, you had to lick your finger and touch wood or something would happen (I can't remember). So one time I farted, went to touch the front of my scooter, hit the tin can, and cut my finger so bad I had to go to the ER to get it stitched. (Of course, another clumsy incident.) One of the moms who lived across from us had been I think a PE coach and was very athletic and one year had us make wet suits and go skin diving. We used to like to go to

Big Corona and Little Corona because the water was so clear. One time her family took us to Catalina Island on their sailboat. On the way there, the winds really picked up and damn near threw her off the boat, while she was trying to get us all into the underneath cabin. Catalina was awesome to go skin diving because the water was so clear. Sometimes friends would take me to. Catalina island on their private boats.

Once or twice we went there as Boy Scouts camping. At the beginning of every summer, we would go on a weeklong or ten-day hike into the sierras as Boy Scouts and have a great time. Bob of course was the leader, and he and I would have a great time. One year we had a kid named Berry, and we started calling him Blubbering Barry because he was crying like a baby because he had bought new boots but didn't break them in, so he got blisters and started crying, so Bob and I called him Blubbering Berry; Tag, the scoutmaster, didn't think it was very funny! But we did. We would also play capture the flag, which was a blast. One year on Catalina, when I was pretty young, we—Bob and I and maybe some friends—crawled under a barbwire fence to explore, and I think we came along some wild hogs, so we started running, and I was so damn blind (I didn't like wearing glasses) that I got tangled up in the barbwire because it came up before I could see it. I was all beat up; but Bob, thank God, helped me out before those damn hogs got me.

BA! No, he took us to a cheap fast-food place and bought me and Bob the smallest hamburger they had and small fries and Coke. I remember getting home, and we were both starving after that big meal, so my mom gave us leftovers for dinner, and she was not happy with our manager. Growing up, my dad made good money, but he wanted us to work and pay for our own cars. I was a paper boy when I was around eleven or twelve, and I actually liked it because it was just throwing papers to a few streets on Lido. I remember on a certain day they would give us papers to throw to people who were not customers. Well, one day I felt a little lazy; so instead of wrapping them up with a large rubber band, I took the easier softer method and threw the whole bundle, probably around fifty papers, into the Newport bay. The problem was the manager was driving by, and as luck would have it, he saw them drifting along the bay with the current. I don't think I lost my job, but he wasn't very happy. Another time he would have us knock on people's doors to see if they would want to subscribe to the paper. He told my mom that he would buy us dinner when we were finished. So after two or so hours, he took us to an expensive place to eat.

The year after I graduated from high school, in August, I came up with the mumps. I ran a high fever, and the doctor said, "When the fever leaves, he will be okay." So maybe after a week, the fever broke, and the next day I felt so good I took the little Honda 50 and rode it to the high school to watch the football team practice. I got home and didn't feel good, so I lay back down on my bed. My mom checked on me and found out I had a very high fever, so my parents took me to the emergency room, where they found that the mumps went down on me. That means that for a male, your testicles swell up so badly that you can't walk or stand, because they are so huge. That can cause infertility. Well, I would find out that my sperm was dead, when a doctor did a sperm count on me. This really upset me because I loved children and always wanted one to twelve kids of my own. Ha-ha. One would be enough.

My first job was working in the summer at a Dairy Queen or a fast food similar to Dairy Queen that was located on Balboa Boulevard, at the beginning of the peninsula. I remember the best part of the job was all the cute girls who would come in! Another job I had when I was around fifteen was at a place called the Blue Dolphin, a restaurant similar to Denny's, and it was near the bridge that led to Lido Isle. My first day, they called me in at around 5:00 p.m., and the place was overflowing because of some large local event that had taken place. I was a dishwasher and busboy, and I think I got home like at one in the morning. I remember my mom saying I smelled so bad that she made me take off my clothes outside.

4

High School to College

One summer, unfortunately for my mom, a cousin named Leslie stayed with us. Without my mom agreeing to it, my dad had told my aunt that "we" would watch Leslie for the summer, and that would pay off a debt my dad owed to his sister (the same sister who took two and a half acres of land as a promissory note that my dad never paid back, so she got the land). Well, this cousin was a spoiled, rotten little girl who was around twelve or thirteen; and I believe after one day, my mom was ready to shoot my dad for agreeing to have my mom take care of her for the summer. All she did was antagonize my brother Mike, and she drove both Mike and my mom insane. But Mike would get back at her also by always saying, "They're making a nest in your hair! They're making a nest in your hair!" insinuating that rats were making a nest in her hair because it was long and curly and unkempt. She was also overweight, so Mike would tease her about that also.

We always had nicknames for the neighbors, and the people who moved into my mom's dream house were a strange couple with a son similar to the age of Chris, the youngest in our family. I don't think my mom liked them much, not just because they lived in her home, but their son was mean to Chris. Well, her nickname was Big Forehead Lady, because she had a big forehead.

I had so much fun with my brother; but when we got older, I sort of became a pest, I think, because he didn't always want his little brother hanging around. One of his first cars was an old Volkswagen van, and man, did he fix it up. The whole inside was wood paneling. He was so good at making things. I couldn't saw a piece of wood straight without damn near cutting off my hand.

One of the first cars I bought was made in France, or maybe Bob bought it and he sold it to me. I bought some kind of little sedan that was red, and my senior year, some of the football players would get together without the coaches, and we would practice without them.

I had a great time in high school and had a lot of friends by the time I was a sophomore. I was always the class clown, from elementary school through high school, and it was evident my freshman year. I was a little crazy also! My freshman English teacher was a woman, and it was her first year teaching! Big mistake with me in the class. Within the first week, I started off by making spitballs and flicking with my finger to her backside when she was writing on the blackboard. By the time the class was over, she was covered from head to toe with spitballs and never knew it. Well, the next day I was called into the office, and evidently someone probably saw her back and realized what had happened, and of course they knew who to blame. Needless to say, that was the end of my spitball career as a student.

I never got good grades. I don't think I spent an hour a week on homework. Homework, what the hell is homework when you can watch TV like *Mork & Mindy* or *Laugh-In*. Now those shows taught you more than school. I remember the first time the Beatles appeared on *The Ed Sullivan Show*, and my dad was outraged. How the hell can they have those hippies on the TV singing songs that make no sense? My dad was notorious for taking naps on the couch, while the rest of the family watched TV.

Bob was always very mechanical and would always be buying or building something or working on his car. Well, one time he ordered a blowgun that shot out BB pellets, and when he first got it, he "accidentally" broke a few windows in the neighborhood. But the best story, there was a really fat kid. Bob was probably sixteen, and this kid was probably eighteen or nineteen. Well, Bob snuck around the corner and hit this kid in the butt. The kid turned around and couldn't find out where it came from. This went on for probably five or six shots, and he finally saw Bob. (I can tell you that if you got hit, it hurt like you had been shot with a gun.) This kid was so big. He got on top of my brother, and I thought he was suffocating him because he was so fat. I started yelling for my dad, and he came running to see what the commotion was. One of the dads in the neighborhood also came. Well, Bob wasn't getting suffocated, and he really couldn't fight the kid because he was under all this blubber, so Bob was joking around and got a hold of this kid's shoes and tied them together, so when he got up, he tripped and fell on his ass. Well, that was the end of the so-called fight, and my dad really got on me for acting like Bob was being killed.

One day I decided to drive my car to the practice field and was chasing everyone. Our quarterback was Alvin White, a great quarterback. Shit, he could throw the ball fifty yards on his knees. One day after we had practiced, he came up with an idea. "Hey, Rat, let's give you a Mohawk haircut." Of course I said hell yes, but they actually shaved the sides with a razor blade and were cutting the hell out of my scalp. I said, "You guys need to stop," and a friend said, "Don't worry, Rat. He is almost done with your haircut."

All through high school, I barely passed; and by my senior year, I had to take an outside class in order to have enough units to graduate. The amazing thing is my last semester, I showed my parents the potential I had, since I made the honor roll. We were eating dinner as usual (we would always have dinner as a family unit), and my mom said, "Look at the paper, Frank, your son Patrick made the honor roll."

My father's eyes rolled. He looked at the paper and then asked to see my report card. Well, this time his eyes did not roll; and I thought he was going to roll over laughing, because he said, "Hell, Ruth, he made the honor roll because he got three As as a PE assistant!"

She said, "I do not care. He made the honor roll," and that was that. I did miraculously graduate from high school, by the skin of my teeth.

By the time I was a sophomore, my friends were driving and buying cars or their parents would buy them cars. When that occurred was when we really started partying on the weekends. It seemed like a lot of the time I would drive. A lot of my friends played other sports besides football, so some of them didn't party like me and Jim, a very close friend. He played football as an offensive tackle but wasn't that great, but in his eyes, he would have started if the guy in front of him wasn't an all-American! His claim to fame a few years later was that the head coach liked him so much that when we were having a team meeting, he took a clipboard and broke it off on top of Jim's head. What a memory for him! We would go to basketball games always together because we liked to get drunk before the game even started. Sometimes we would drink beer, and other times we would drink cheap wine, but we would be pretty drunk going into the game, and I could not handle my drinking like Jim, so by the halftime when we would go out to the car for more, we would come back, and I would be stumbling all over the place. Everyone, including the coaches, cheer leaders, and fans, knew once again that Pat was drunker than hell.

My freshman year we were dressing up for football practice, and a good friend looked at my toes and said, "Shit, look at Pat's toes. They are so long, they look like rat claws." To this day, my nickname is still Rat. In high school, we gave all our friends nicknames, like Dog for Smitty Dog, or R for Reynolds, or E for Easterling; but nobody had a nickname of Rat! I always thought the girls in high school weren't attracted to me because they thought they named me Rat because I looked like a rat. Can you believe from my freshman year to my senior year I did not have *one* date the entire four years? Not even for my senior prom. When my friends would go to proms, I would always find someone to hang out with and get shit-faced drunk. Looking back at it, I think it probably kept me from doing something stupid to myself.

Later when I got older, I would think about killing myself, but I would usually get so drunk that I would pass out and that would keep me from doing it. One time when I lived in Bakersfield, I was driving down a street with a big cliff on one side, and I drove my car to go off the cliff, but I hit a curb, and it slung my car in the opposite direction. I was so blind I had to wear glasses to play football, and many times they would fog up or fall off my face, and then I could barely see the fingers on my hand. My freshman year I had tried wearing contact lenses, but my eyes would not adjust to them, and all they did was cause a lot of discomfort, so after a few weeks of trying them, I gave up and just wore my glasses.

My junior year they had come up with soft contact lenses, but they were not approved by the FDA yet, but my doctor was able to get them for me. They actually felt great, and there was no discomfort, so I thought this will be great. I won't have to wear glasses anymore, especially playing football. You had to always make sure to take them off before going to bed, because if you keep them in while you were sleeping, it could cause a lot of damage to your eyes. Well, one night I got drunk and came home and forgot that I even had them on. So I went to bed, and when I woke up, I was totally blind. I could not see anything. So I yelled for my mom and dad and told them. They got a hold of my eye doctor, and he told them to meet him at his office. Like I said, I forgot that I was even wearing them, so he had to put fluids into my eye to get them out, because they had stuck to my eyes and drained a lot of the fluid out of my eyes, and that is why I couldn't see. He got them out, and I still couldn't see very well, so he prescribed a lot of different drops for me to take and said to come back and see him that coming Monday. By Monday, my vision had almost come back when I went to see him. He told me and my parents I was very fortunate because I could have lost my vision permanently. I was so scared about losing my vision, I stopped wearing them and went back to my glasses.

At the end of fall practice and two-a-days for football, somehow I got talked into getting a Mohawk haircut. Our quarterback, Alvin White, a.k.a. Big Al, was the barber; and he made sure he did a very professional job using a razor blade to cut very close on the back and sides of my head. Now I don't think Al had a shaking problem, but when they let me look in the mirror, my head was a bloody mess. I think Al thought I was going to pass out, and so he handed me a bottle of whisky someone had given him and said something like

"Rat, little buddy, don't worry. Take a shot of this to calm down." He knew I liked to drink! I have one of those pencils that will stop all the bleeding in no time. But after he had stopped the bleeding, my head was now full of giant blood clots, and it looked like I had been scalped. Thank God I had a baseball cap, so I put it on. When I got home, I thought nobody would notice the blood, although I had a pretty good buzz, so I'm sure my judgment wasn't too good.

When I walked in the door, of course my mom happened to be in the living room, and she looked at me kind of strange. She said, "Patrick, my god, it looks like your head has been bleeding. Take off the cap so I can get a better look." Well, when I took it off, I really thought she was going to pass out. All she could say was "Patrick, Patrick, what have you done now? Oh my god, my god, you are scheduled to have your senior picture taken tomorrow. Oh my god, my god…" Then a pause. "Oh my god, Patrick, your father is home!"

My dad took one look and went crazy. "Goddamn it! Do you have one brain cell left in that damn brain of yours?? You look like something out of a science fiction movie. What the hell! Were you going to finally think this was going to get you a date!"

I was so upset. I went into my room, got some money, put a few clothes in a duffel bag, and walked out the door. I was running away at the age of eighteen and never returning home. I caught a bus on Pacific Coast Highway, and I think I got all the way to Redondo Beach or Santa Monica. I got off the bus, not having a clue where I was going to go, and I didn't have enough money to get a hotel for one night. I was standing there, and a man came up to me and said, "Son, it looks like you're pretty upset. Are you having a tough day?" I said yes, I just decided I was going to leave my house and live on my own. He said, "Something must have really upset you to run away."

I said yes, my dad and I had a few words, and I was tired of hearing him yell at me. I said my dad flipped out when he saw my new haircut I got for football. With that, I took off my cap, and he had the look my mom had when I thought she was going to pass out. He said something like "My god, son, have rats been gnawing on your head?" and then he just burst out laughing. He then said, "Son, put that cap back on before you cause a traffic accident." He went on,

"Now I know why your dad got upset. I will tell you what, do you have enough money to make it back to Newport?"

I said, "I'm not sure, to be honest."

Then he said, "I will tell you what, I will pay for your return trip to go back to Newport because it doesn't appear you have any other options."

I said, "Wow, thank you."

He also gave me a dollar or two and said, "You smell like alcohol. You can buy yourself something to eat and then get on the next bus to Newport." He said, "Don't worry, your dad will get over it; but just a suggestion, when you know he is home, I would suggest you keep that hat on," and then again he burst out laughing.

Well, I got home probably around one in the morning. Thank God the next day was a Saturday. My mom was up waiting for me and opened up the front door to let me in. She said, "Patrick, don't worry about your dad being mad. As soon as he left, I didn't think I was going to be able to make him stop laughing. I'm not sure if I have ever seen your father laugh so hard and for so long. When he stopped, he said, 'My god, I knew Pat was crazy, but he outdid himself this time.'" Then he told my mom, "He is the craziest son we have. I hope he makes it to his twenty-first birthday."

The next morning I woke up a little startled, and the first thing I remembered was *Oh my god, I'm supposed to pick up a few friends and go to the high school football all-star game at the junior college. Man, there is no way I'm going to go to that game where there are at least fifteen thousand people in the stands and let them see my new haircut.* Well, I picked my friends up after all, and we partied for a while before going to the game, and needless to say, they convinced me that if I wore my hat, nobody would even see my Mohawk. So we went ahead and went to the game. We got in, and we were about to the middle of the stadium bleachers when one of my friends had a brilliant idea and, before I knew it, ripped my hat off and threw it down onto the field. My perception at that moment was that all fifteen thousand fans shut up, and there was not a peep in that stadium. And then five seconds later, they were all laughing so hard you would have thought it was a George Carlin concert. I ran as fast as I could to my car and got in it and started drinking beer as fast as I could. I guess my friends said when they got to the car after the game, I was passed out, so they drove me home.

When I was a senior, all my friends knew I was a virgin; so a few of us went to Tijuana, Mexico, to get drunk and to find me a hooker. Well, I succeeded, but the problem was I wanted more sex, and she said I had to pay more. I was very drunk and caused a commotion, so a few Mexicans threw me out of the bar, with my pants still hanging down on my shoes.

I have to mention that Bob was two years in front of me in school because I was held back, so when I was a freshman, he was a junior. I believe I mentioned earlier he was a gifted athlete and was starting as a running back for his B football team, which was considered the way to go to varsity the next year. Everyone thought that he had a good chance of starting his senior year as a running back for the varsity team. Since he was such a good athlete and naturally strong, he didn't have to try nearly as hard as the blind ostrich. The summer of his senior year, he worked full-time at the airport, and his off time would be spent mostly with his friends flying to different airstrips and sometimes staying the night and leaving the next day. Due to this fact, he did not attend the workouts they were having daily at the high school. Even though my brother in my opinion and many others thought that he would start that year, the coach took a disliking to the fact that even though he was in great shape when he came for two-a-days, he didn't attend the workouts during the summer. He punished my brother for not attending by not even playing him the entire season. I can't remember if he ever got in for one play. And I can tell you I was so pissed off at the coach that I never wanted to play football again. And once again my brother showed his strength by sitting on the bench for the entire game and never indicating that he was upset. Now you know another reason why he is my hero. What a man at eighteen, to show the coach and others that no matter what he did or said to my brother, he took it with dignity and never complained.

One time my dad and I went on a flight with Bob to land at Big Bear Airport. This might have been when he was still fifteen and a half and didn't have a lot of airtime. So we were flying into Big Bear Airport, and there was a very heavy crosswind that he had never experienced. My dad, having many hours flying, didn't take the controls from the passenger seat but helped give my brother instructions so we had a smooth and gentle landing. It was the same with taking off, maybe more difficult, I can't remember, but Bob did an excellent job, and after that experience, I loved to fly with my brother, because I knew he was an excellent pilot. One thing about my brother, when he wanted to achieve something, nobody or nothing else was going to hold him back; and that still stands to this day. I have always thought of him as my hero, especially when he was a fighter pilot and flew for the Wild Weasels in an F-4 fighter jet. In fact, one of my most cherished experiences with my brother was when he flew back in with the squadron he was with and was the commander of his team after fighting in the Gulf War. When they landed and we all had a big party with everyone in the squadron, his backseat man came up and told us that they would not be here if it wasn't for the fact that Bob was the best fighter pilot he had ever known; and on several occasions, they would have been shot down if it wasn't for his great skills. Talk about being pumped up, I was thinking to myself, *Oh my god, he really is my hero, and I am so fortunate to have him as a brother.* He would go on after retiring as a full commander, just short of being made a general, and flew commercial airplanes and retired from that. All I can say is if I was on a commercial jet that was having any kind of problems, the pilot I would want would be my brother.

I think when I was a freshman, I might have weighed 105 lbs., and so I was very small to play football, plus I was blind as a bat, so not only was I not very coordinated, but I couldn't see, because I tried to play without my glasses (before contacts). The only thing I had going for me was I didn't care how small I was. I would still try to kill the person I was trying to tackle. I think my senior year I might have weighed 138 and was maybe 5'6". My junior year, we got a great new head coach who had been at another high school that I believe was made up of mostly low-income Hispanic kids, and they went to the California Interscholastic Foundation (CIF) playoffs I believe twelve years in a row.

Newport had not been to a playoff game I think since around 1962, so everyone was excited with the new coach. My senior year, I might have weighed 140 lbs. soaking wet and was about 5'6". When we would play a game, even though I was legally blind in one eye and the other eye wasn't much better, I did not want to wear my glasses because I thought people in the stadium would think I looked like a nerd. Well, the other thing was I had a pencil neck and no shoulders and had skinny legs; and so when I ran out onto the field for a game, I probably looked like an ostrich with a football helmet on. Football was pretty much a disaster, because maybe after the first or second game, during a practice I suffered a high ankle sprain, and so was hurt most of the season, although I wouldn't have played much anyway.

I remember one practice, I was on the second team offense against the first string defense. I was an offensive back then, and on that play, I was supposed to take down the defensive tackle who probably weighed around 215 lbs. So I threw my little body at him, and he went down, but I will never forget the coach totally going off on me, saying, "What the hell are you thinking? You could have hurt Jim really bad." Talk about me being pissed inside. I thought, *What the hell are you yelling at me for? This guy outweighs me by probably 75 lbs., and you're pissed at me.* To be honest, even though everyone thought this coach was good, I never really liked him. The coach before him I really liked because he would always say something good about me. Like he would say to some good player, "Goddamn it, why don't you have the desire that McNeese has?"

I remember if you were not in another sport after football season, all the football players would all be in the same PE class at the end of the day. Every few weeks, we would have like a challenge day, and sometimes we would put on 16 oz of boxing gloves and beat each other up. Well, you know me and my nose. By the first round, I would be a bloody mess, and the coaches would say, "Okay, McNeese, that is enough."

And I would be so pissed, almost crying, saying, "No way, I want to keep going."

The coaches would look at themselves and go, "All right, get back in the ring." And I would go the distance, no matter how much I was bleeding. I think that is why the head varsity coach and staff liked me, because I would never, never give up, no matter how big the guy was.

When I was a junior, we were doing tackling drills without pads or helmets. A guy would be in a designated box, and he was supposed to stay inside that box, while the other guy tried to run through him. It came my turn. I might have weighed 130 lbs., and the guy I was going against was a starting linebacker on the varsity team and probably weighed at least 185 lbs. I tried to run through his box, and he basically picked me up and slammed me to the ground. The next thing I remember was the coaches were over me saying, "Get up, McNeese, get up." I guess I had been completely knocked out, and when I tried to stand up, I fell back down on the back of my head and was out again. I never will forget how worried the coaches were that my parents would raise hell, and they would get into deep trouble with the CIF committee. Well, my dad, being my dad, said, "No way, no one is ever going to find out about this, so you have nothing to worry about."

Back then, no one really knew the significance of head injuries, but my doctor was ahead of his time. This was my second serious head injury within the past six months (one from a car accident). He convinced my parents that okay, I can still play football (although he really didn't want me to play my junior or senior year), but he said, "No way is he going to play next year" (my junior year). I was devastated. My mom said I sat in our patio and cried for hours, because I would not be able to play the next year. The wrestling coaches were always trying to get me to go out for wrestling because they knew I was a tough kid, and I guess with that sport, you don't have to really see that good, and you're against someone your same size. I didn't go out for wrestling because I was always trying everything I could to gain weight, and they wanted me to wrestle at the weight I was at.

When I was a junior, my dad decided he didn't like being an insurance agent, although he made a lot of money; so according to my mom, he might as well give his business to a guy he shared his office with, because I guess he didn't get much money for giving him his clients. He decided to go back to USC and get his master's degree in hospital administration, and I remember typing his thesis when I was a senior. To try to make ends meet, he substituted teaching in local high schools as a PE coach. In fact, he would teach at the same high school I went to, and all the coaches really liked my dad. Remember my dad had been an ex-fighter, so he could still take care of himself if he needed to. But one morning out of the blue, during a PE class, a kid kicked him so hard in the groin that he was swollen and black and blue and laid up in bed for a day or two. Well, by the end of the day, everyone knew who the kid was; and the coaches knew I was mad as hell. So the next morning before the first period started, they let the kid into the locker rooms and had everyone else leave. I was waiting for him, and the coaches watched me beat the hell out of this kid. I think they had to drag me off him. I was so pissed off. How could a kid have no respect and kick a coach in the groin?

My dad never would listen to my mom when it came to money, and so that is why I'm probably not a "trust fund" baby, which in hindsight is a good thing because I probably would be dead and not writing about myself. My dad would lose both houses on Lido, and in addition, my mom had received two or two and a half acres of land her mom gave her in a will. Well, my dad would get a loan from his sister and give the two and a half acres to her as a promissory note that he never kept, so she got the land. The last year or two on Lido, we would rent a house a few doors down from the one we lived in. It really was a bummer for my mom, because she lost her dream home; and if he had listened to her, they probably could have saved it with some intelligent financing.

My sophomore year was the beginning of my head injuries. I was driving Bob home from his work, and a guy ran a red light and broadsided us. I was knocked out, and my brother didn't have his seat belt on, so luckily he was thrown to the floor but damn near lost one of his ears, from being cut so bad. I will never forget my brother saying he dragged me out of the car and was yelling at the guy, "Do you have a blanket?" The guy was Asian and didn't speak much English because all he kept yelling back to my brother was "New car, new car, new car!" The ambulance came, and my brother told them to take us to Hoag Hospital, but they took us to a new hospital in Costa Mesa and reportedly got kickbacks for doing that. Well, I was really injured badly, with my nose on the side of my face, a severe head injury, and three or four broken ribs. I was out of it in the ER, but my mom and dad I guess came running in, not knowing if I was alive. The doctor came in, and I guess the first thing he asked my parents was "Is his nose always like that, or is it broken?"

My mom went crazy and said, "Get this friggin' idiot doctor out of here and transfer my son to Hoag." I stayed in the hospital for five or seven days recovering, mostly from my head trauma at the hospital that I was taken to.

I was a little crazy, so shortly after the second head injury, I was with a friend and decided to get on a bus, while the kids were getting off from school. I ran to the back, opened the emergency door, and jumped out the back of the bus. Very funny, but unfortunately for me, the driver was the wife of the varsity football team's offensive and defensive backs' coach. The next morning I was walking into school, and he met me. Yes, the coach, and he threw me up against a wall and said, "If I knew you still weren't recovering from a head injury, I would beat the hell out of you right now!" Once again, I would never run through a bus again!

By the time I was a junior, I was getting drunk pretty much every weekend, except during football season, and I think I would even drink then, watching the varsity team play.

I was a Dr. Jekyll and Mr. Hyde when it came to my drinking even in high school. I would be either the funny one or the one who wanted to fight anyone who wanted to fight me.

I think if you talked to my friends back then, they would tell you I was the original rapper. Why? Because for some unknown reason, one night we were partying at a friend's house, with his parents, and I picked up their phone and yelled at everyone, "Shut up, shut up, the Lord has called," and then I started rapping. For example, I would start with friends' names. "Dale, my god, you look pale. Is your date going stale? What do you think no fire, because there is hail… Well, don't wait for the mail…you will surely fail…and please don't get so drunk that we have to post bail!" A friend's nickname. "R, are you driving your dad's sports car? Well, remember we are too young to go to a bar. But look, I have some whisky in this jar…and it's stronger than anything you would find at a bar… Just please after you drink, don't drive your dad's car… Not near or far…

"Mike…you're smart. You rode your bike… Don't worry, nobody is going to think you're a little tike… But I promise you if I drink much more, I might have to hitchhike…

"Dog…I know you're drunk…but please don't call Linder a hog… She will hit you so hard, you will think you're in a fog. You will be barking up the wrong tree… And I promise you she will hit you so hard that you will have to pee…so please don't flee, just stay here and be.

"Stubbies, where are you? Upstairs passed out in a room, in a closet with the broom, or, Stub, are you lying in the tub…or once again are you in your car, with the heater on, and your brain is gone!

"Jim, we know you like to chug…but do you always have to puke on someone's rug! Come on, no wonder no one wants to give you a hug… We know you drink, but you're not a thug… You just like to finish your jug…but don't get angry with that look on your mug… Come on, give us all a big hug!"

Another signature calling card was when I would say BA! I have no idea where I got it, but when I made people laugh at the end, I would always yell out BA! Even my dad would crack up, and when friends were over our house sometimes, he would look at me and go BA! And everyone would crack up.

One night when I was a senior, I went to a nooner (daytime high school party) and came home around 5:00 p.m. and was so drunk my mom said, "Patrick, get the hell out of here before your dad comes home, and don't come back until you're sober." That was one of my worst drunks in high school. I would later go to a party that night, which was a junior college party. I already had a reputation as being crazy and liking to fight, so someone opened the door, and a couple of college guys saw me and I guess beat the hell out of me. Somehow I was found passed out in the bushes at our high school. They drove me home, and instead of going to my bedroom through a private door, I went through the front door, which meant I had to go through my parents' room to get to my room. I got disoriented, and they found me getting sicker than a dog in their walk-in closet, my god. They took me in bed; and I guess I was throwing up in my sleep, while I was lying on my back, choking to death. They took me to the hospital where they diagnosed me with alcohol poison and said I was lucky to be alive. The next morning my dad had me up and cleaning out their closet, which made me more sick, so he gave up and had me go back to bed. It affected me so bad that it took at least two months for me to start drinking again. I would look at alcohol and start getting sick.

When I was twenty, my dad was offered a job as the director of a regional center in Bakersfield, which he accepted. I think Bob, Jane, and I thought, *Okay, this is the time for Mom to finally leave Dad. She is not going to move to Bakersfield and leave Newport.* To our surprise, she did, and later she told me she would not leave him until both Mike and Chris were raised. She did finally leave him when Chris was around twelve, and to her complete and sad surprise, both Mike and Chris decided to live with my dad, and I think deep down this really hurt my mom. Even though she may have said something to my sister, she never let me know. The one great thing my dad taught us from a very early age was not to judge anyone by the color of their skin, their race, their religion, or anything else that might be different. And he proved he did not have a prejudiced bone in his body when he hired the first Asian and black doctor in Bakersfield. What a great example to have as a dad, and to this day, I have tried my best never to judge anyone different than me, and I think I followed his example to a T when I married a Mexican. I can tell you this was the first girlfriend I introduced to my dad, and instantly I could tell he fell in love with her. I introduced him to Ivy when he was in the VA hospital in the desert. It turned out that both he and Lou (my dad's wife) loved Ivy and especially Little Ivy. I am sure he met Deli, but I don't remember when.

My senior year after football season, I started working at my brother-in-law's hardware store. This was way before superstores like

Home Depot came into existence. This store was probably one of the biggest in Orange County, and it happened to be one of my favorite jobs. I would wind up being the guy who would replace the screening in screen doors and windows, and it was my favorite job at the store, and Darryl's dad let me do all the screening for the customers. One time I was trying to come into the front door holding a screen door, and the door closed on me (heavy glass), and my hand went through the door. Well, I didn't realize it, but Darryl saw what happened, and I guess my one thumb was dangling off my hand. So I was rushed to the newly opened hospital, and they sewed it back on. The problem was a few days later, it got badly infected because they hadn't cleaned it good enough, so they had to reopen it and clean it and sew it back up. I can tell you even after being numbed with Novocain, it still hurt like hell.

5

Events in My Twenties and Thirties

Bob and I never really had an all-out brawl against each other, but when I was nineteen or twenty, I think I should plead temporary insanity. Why? Because we both were conservative and pro-Vietnam War, but Bob was trying to decide if he wanted to fly for the marines or the air force. As I said earlier, I knew how to push his buttons. By this time, we were both grown men, and I was probably 5'10" and weighed 170 lbs., and he was probably 5'8" and weighed 180. Anyway, he was working on his car in the garage, and I said, "What the hell is going on, Jarhead!"

He got up and said, "What the hell did you call me?"

I said, "You heard me. What the hell are you up to, Jarhead!"

He told me, "Call me that again and I'm going to beat the hell out of you."

I went, "So you're going to beat me up if I call you a jarhead." With that, he hit me with a right that knocked me down. I got up and said, "What the hell! Is that all you have?"

He went, "You will find out what I have if you call me that again!"

I said, "So if I call you a jarhead, you're going to hit me!" Well, he smacked me to the ground again.

By this time, my mom and sister heard all the noise in the garage and came running out and said, "What is going on?"

I said, "Bob doesn't like his new name!"

My mom said, "Patrick, what are you doing?" because I think I might have been bleeding a little by the second punch.

I said, "Every time I call Bob a jarhead, he hits me."

She said, "Goddamn it, quit calling him a jarhead."

I said, "But, Mom, Bob is a jarhead." With that, he hit me again, and down I went. By this time, everyone was yelling, "Defend yourself! Don't just let him hit you."

I said, "But look, the jarhead can't hurt me." With that, once again he hit me. The whole time, I would not defend myself. Finally I started running down the street while they were all in the garage, and I was yelling, "There is a jarhead in our garage!"

Well, he caught up to me, tackled me in the street, pinned me down, and said, "Don't say that again."

By this time, I think both of us had lost it because I said, "You going to hit me while you have me pinned, Jarhead!" Yep, he hit me; and by this time, the whole neighborhood was damn near watching, including Mr. Perry, who was yelling at me, "For god's sake, Pat, defend yourself!"

When I turned twenty-one, my friend Dale had my party at his house, and his parents were there along with my best friends. They really got a kick out of me and Jim trying to outchug each other. Well, if I got drunk enough on beer, there was a good chance I was going to get sick and throw up. Unfortunately that night, I did get sick, but it was all over a very expensive velvet (I think) chair. To my surprise, I wasn't so drunk that I saw his parents were not angry but laughing. So I thought the best thing to do to get sober was to jump off their dock and go for a swim. Not a good idea at all! I jumped in the bay and was so drunk I forgot how to swim. That I think is pretty drunk, and fortunately for me, a few of my friends saw that I was sinking, so they dove in with all their clothes on and pulled me up to the dock. It was still a great party that I will never forget, and I still think of how kind Dale's parents were. Well, Stubs, who was notorious for passing out in a room and us trying to find him, did not pass out in a room that night. We found him in his car, with all the windows up, passed out in the car and sweating like a bullet. So we or they pulled him out of the car and got him sober enough to drive home in his new Ford Pinto.

When my parents moved to Bakersfield, I was twenty years old and moved into a small bachelor apartment that was on the same property that my brother-in-law and sister lived on along with his parents in the back house. At that time, I had gotten a job working for a construction company, Warmington Development, as the superintendent's assistant, or gopher. The Warmington brothers liked me and actually watched after me. It was a great company, and the father was well known for building custom homes in LA and Pasadena, but this was their first tract home development consisting of townhomes. The family consisted of two sets of twins, and Bob and Jim were taking over for their dad in the construction business. The superintendent was a great guy also, and young, and had been raised in Big Bear. Both the brothers and Wil, the superintendent, had gorgeous wives. Sometimes they would have me over for dinner; and I was like, yes, I want what they have. They also had been raised on Lido Isle and had gone to USC.

One time while I worked for them, my friends and I had been at a party on Lido, and I had to take a pee. Well, I pulled over and went into the bushes to pee, not knowing there was a family across the street with their kids, who were in college, playing pool in their garage. I guess they got pissed off at me because I was pissing in the bushes across the street from where they were. So two or three of them came across the street, gave me a bad time, and beat the hell out of me, while two or three of my friends stayed in the car and watched me get the hell beat out of me. My parents and other friends were so pissed off the next day that they didn't help me out. Well, once again I had a concussion. I will never forget, because Bob or Jim had been raised in a house just a few doors from them and knew the family. They were so angry; they told me what to do. So I did what they told me; and I got a bag, filled it with dog poop, set it on the porch of the people who had beaten me up, lit it on fire, and rang the doorbell. Well, at least someone had a shoe or shoes full of dog poop. BA. We used to have a great time at the job site also. I would be close with the foreman of the job, also a young guy, and they taught me to drink "black" coffee in the morning and have a few beers after work on Fridays. I really looked up to these guys because they were young but successful. When they gave me a job to do, like place a fiberglass tub in a bathroom, I felt like I was one of the construction workers. It really built up my confidence and self-esteem working for them.

I also was working at a five-star restaurant in Newport Beach that overlooked the Newport Beach Pier called the Alley West. Both jobs were great, and I really liked them both. I mostly worked as a glorified busboy at the Alley West and was hopeful they would train me to become a bartender. I had two good friends who also worked there, Mike and Jim (Bones). The owner of the Alley West sort of had the same theme as the playboys, and all the girls who worked there were out-and-out foxes. They were beautiful, and we had so much fun working. Some weekends, we would set a theme, like one night we pretended that we were the Beverly hillbillies. The customers would have no idea what was going on, but we would be cracking up back in the kitchen. Everybody really got along well, and my idol became the head bartender whose name was Mike. He had a gorgeous girlfriend and might have been around twenty-eight or twenty-nine when I was twenty or twenty-one. One day some old people who had been at a funeral came in and were seated at the bar.

They started to get pretty hammered, so the bartender kept an eye on them. Well, when they were about to leave, the one old lady got sicker than a skunk and threw up underneath the bar under the stool. They left, and I was left to clean up the mess. A few minutes later, one of the old men came in and asked if we had found the lady's false teeth. Well, I was just beginning to clean up the puke, and there they were in with the vomit. It was sick, but we all were just laughing our butts off. We had some crazy times there. It was known for having the best abalone around, and its market price was always expensive even back then. I loved abalone, and sometimes people would order it for the first time and not like it. I didn't care if they had bitten into it or not. When their plates went to the dishwasher, I would eat up the leftover abalone before he had a chance to clean the plate. They also had a downstairs wine cellar/room with some very expensive wines. One time a customer came in, and they went down to the wine room and ordered the most expensive wine we had. The owner was a little weary because he was not sure if they could afford it. So he billed them before they opened up the bottle, and yep, they paid for it. I had never seen anyone pay that much for a bottle of wine, and that was in the early '70s.

One night I was just getting off work and was walking past the Newport pier when I heard all kinds of yelling. So I walked on the pier and found out that a couple, man and woman, were three-fourths of the way up the pier; and some idiot pushed them into the ocean. Well, these clowns on the pier yelling had no clue what to do. They were trying to get people to take off their belts so they could dangle them down to the couple. Hell, this was at least twelve or one in the morning, and there were no lifeguards to be found. The woman had wrapped herself around one of the pier pilings and was getting really beat up. She did not know how to swim. All I could think of was jump in after her. So I ran off the pier and stripped down to my boxers, and I went after the lady, while a friend went after the guy. I got to the woman, and she was hysterical. I told her to let go of the piling and grab on to me while I would swim her to shore. Well, she grabbed on to me all right and literally started to make me go underwater. Thank God I remembered what to do; so I swam under her, grabbed her from the back, and grabbed a hold of her shoulders from the back and dragged her to shore. The surf wasn't really big, but it was pitch dark, and I was exhausted by the time I reached shore. And halfway to shore, the lifeguards showed up and at least turned on a big floodlight so I could see the waves coming as I went to shore. I will never forget, because the next day, for the first time in my life, I was in the local paper for saving her life. None of my friends or family could believe it. Thank God I wasn't drunk that night, or I probably would have drowned along with this lady.

When I was around twenty-one, my friend worked at a restaurant bar that was owned by a producer or director from Hollywood, and he was just a great guy. Well, he had gotten hold of a copy of *The Exorcist* when it first came out and was going to be showing it exclusively at his place, so one Saturday or Sunday, we were all there drinking and having a good time. We were talking to Jed, and one of his employees that I think he had fired started giving him a hard time. I told the guy to leave him alone and to give me a hard time, if he was looking for a fight. The next thing I knew, I believe he hit the back of my head with a beer mug, and out I went. I would wake up at Hoag Hospital with a major head injury and concussion. I would wind up being in the hospital for a month, and some of the tests back then were god awful and very painful. One test was they strapped you to a chair—I thought it was an electric chair—and they inserted a spinal tap into your spine and have a bubble of air go to the top of your brain. They would start with you sitting straight, then you would face the ceiling, then you would be upside down, and then you would face the ceiling again and then back sitting straight. I don't know how long it took, but it seemed like hours, and I remember screaming at the top of my lungs. I was in so much pain. I will never forget that stay in the hospital, because I wasn't sure if I would ever get out. I remember friends visiting, and I was all drugged up because of pain, and they would sneak in a six-pack of beer, and I would say, "Hell yes, I'd rather have a beer than the crap they are putting in me. All it does is space me out."

Because of the serious head injury, I decided along with the doctors and my parents to move up to Bakersfield to recover. I will never forget because my mom said for the first three months all I did was eat and feed the cat, and she watched us both get fat. During that time, I decided to go back to college and went out for the junior college football team. They had one of the top programs in the nation and a stadium that held around twenty thousand people. I was really excited about school and about football, because I was now 5'10" and weighed around 190 lbs. (I grew a lot after high school). From the first time I met the head coach, we seemed to really get along. He loved the fact that I had played for Ernie Johnson, my high school coach who now coached a junior college team in Southern California. From the very beginning of spring practice, the coaches liked my skills, especially as a free safety and knowing where to be at the right time. I was also doing very well in school, for the first time.

When Easter break came, I came down to Costa Mesa and stayed with my sister and brother-in-law. My parents and Mike and Chris also came down for Easter weekend to visit my sister and the grandkids and me. I had met up all my friends that week and found out that they were having a huge party on Easter Sunday. On Easter morning, I got dressed to go to mass with my dad and the rest of the family. After I got all dressed up that Sunday morning, the phone rang. It was a friend asking where I was! I said I was getting ready to go to mass. He said, "Pat, don't you remember the party that all the local bars and restaurants are putting on at the Orange County raceway? You're supposed to pick me up." So the next thing my family knew was I was now in a tank top and shorts.

My dad looked at me and said, "You're not going to church looking like that."

And I said, "You're right. I no longer live under your roof, and I'm going to a huge party and missing church." Needless to say, he was not to happy.

Well, this party, which consisted of all the big restaurants in Newport and the surrounding areas, was huge with a massive number of people. We got there and had a great time. I got really drunk but still had a great time. It was probably around four or five, and I decided I better get home. So I got in my Volkswagen and started heading off to the freeway on a dirt road. Something clicked; and I think I was going around sixty miles an hour when I remembered I was supposed to take my friend, whom I had picked up, home. Well, this Volkswagen was not a porch, but I guess I tried to do a U-turn going sixty. The people said all they saw was this bug flipping around and around until it settled, and you could not see it because of all the dust. All I remember was coming to and thinking the car was on fire. I just had on shorts, a tank top, and flip-flops; but I tried kicking the back window out. I didn't have my seat belt on, and I guess I wound up in the back seat. I made it out of the car and saw people running toward me and driving toward me. I remember saying to myself, *Thank God I didn't wreak my car*, because it was on its hood, but the wheels were spinning around, and the stereo was going.

The people said they saw me fall facedown and thought for sure I was dead. Well, I wasn't, but some people put me in their Porsche and rushed me to the hospital, where once again I would have a concussion. When I got back to school that Monday, I went to football practice and told the coach what happened, so I didn't practice much the rest of the spring. Near the end of the semester, the coach called me into his office and asked what I planned on doing during the summer. I said I was going to go down to Newport and work down there. He suggested he could get me a good job for the summer, and that way I would stay out of trouble going down to Newport. I told him that being a beach kid, there was no way I could stay in the heat of Bakersfield during the summer, so I decided to move back down there that summer. Well, my dad was so pissed. He said, "We are not driving you down there to live." I didn't have a car, so he thought I was stranded. That wasn't the case, because I packed up my bags and had my brother drop me off at an on-ramp to the freeway and hitchhiked my way to Newport Beach. I guess I didn't want to stay in Bakersfield.

I actually did okay. I got my first ride from Bakersfield all the way to downtown Sherman Way. And then I got a ride all the way to downtown LA. But the problem was it was getting toward dusk, and I was dropped off in the middle of a black area known as Watts. I finally saw a car pull over, and he let me in. It was a black guy around forty, and he said, "Son, what the hell are you doing in this area?" I told him my story, and he went, "I'm going to give you a ride up until we get into a safe area, and then I will drop you off." So I believe he drove to Torrance and dropped me off at an off-ramp. From there, I made it to Costa Mesa, and that is where my sister picked me up because I was going to move back into the little bachelor pad on her father-in-law's land. I would work at the Alley West that summer and use a friend's bike to get back and forth to work.

When the summer was almost over, I was riding home to my sister's, and it was getting dark. The streets in Costa Mesa had a stop sign at almost every block, so I would check and cruise through most of them without stopping. One that I did not stop at also had a car that didn't stop. So I remember getting hit, and it felt like the bike and I were going under the car, but at the last minute, somehow I got untangled with the bike and got thrown over the car, and it was like slow motion. I remember, *No more head injuries*; so I wrapped my arms around my head, hit the ground with one of my knees, then hit my head and was out cold. I came to, and there were a bunch of people trying to make sure I was okay. They wouldn't let me get up, so I asked one of the guys if he would call my sister and tell her what happened, that I was okay and the paramedics were taking me to the hospital. I got to Hoag Hospital. I had a slight buzz from drinking, and of course my typical reaction in the ER was to tell the nurses how pretty they were, and I was trying to put the make on them. Well, my sister and brother-in-law came in, and my sister saw me trying to put the move on the nurses and almost hit the floor. She was so mad. Not so much at me, but at the guy who called her, because she asked how I was, and he told her, "All I know was that he was still breathing when I was out there next to him," and she wasn't sure if she was going to find me dead or alive.

I would wind up with another concussion and a shattered knee-cap, so they put a full leg cast on me.

I will never forget when I moved to Bakersfield, a couple of the girls who worked at the Alley West said, "Oh, Bakersfield, we had a couple of friends in college that were from Bakersfield. Do you know what the big deal is in Bakersfield on a Friday and Saturday night?"

I said, "No, what?" and they said, "Cruising down Chester Lane, one of the big streets that goes through the main part of the city of Bakersfield," and they started laughing. At that time, I think the population of Bakersfield and the surrounding area was around seventy-five thousand people, and they were right. The big deal was to cruise Chester on Friday and Saturday night.

The first three to six months I was living in Bakersfield, I had not met anyone who was my age (twenty-one or so), and the kids I met were kids who went to high school with Mike. That is the reason I made a lot of good friends with kids who were five and six years younger than me. They all got a kick out of me, listening to my stories about parties that I went to in Newport, plus I could buy their beer legally. One time a guy who would turn out to be a good friend was talking to me at a party, and he asked me what kind of crazy stuff I would do at parties. I said, "See that bathroom over there?" He said yes. "I might just get a little angry and pull the toilet off the floor." With that, he went into the bathroom, took the toilet, and ripped it off the floor, which caused the waterline to come lose and make a flood.

He said to me, "Is that about how you would do it?"

And I said, "Oh my god, yep, that is a good job." Then they were trying to get everyone to leave the house, but I got another great idea. I took the garden hose and started spraying it into the front door so nobody could leave…BA. My reputation began with that party in Bakersfield, and it would continue until I would eventually get sober. One of my earliest crazy times in Bakersfield was when I was with a bunch of guys who played football at Bakersfield Junior College.

One night a bunch of us went to a party we found out about. The problem was they did not want any jocks at their party. This was a big house with probably two oak entry doors that were maybe ten feet tall. I'm not sure what I was thinking, except I was drunk, so I got a running start far enough away that I was running as fast as I could and ran into these doors. I wasn't a 250 lbs. lineman. I probably weighed around 190 lbs., but it was enough to knock one of the doors off its hinges and come down in the interior of the house, just missing a few people. The next day, I found out that it was a local judge who owned the house, and he was not very happy when he found out a player from the junior college had knocked it down. I found out that he wanted to prosecute me for illegal entry or something to that effect. That was serious enough that I could go to prison. This was serious, so a great running back who was with me and I met the judge in his chambers, but luckily the head coach went with us. We were actually waiting in his courtroom while he was in the middle of a case. He saw us and said he was taking a break and called us back to his chambers. The first thing he said was, "Which one of you is responsible for breaking down my door?"

I said, "Sir, I'm sorry, but I broke down your door."

He looked at me in amazement and said, "Son, how much do you weigh?" I told him I weighed around 190 lbs. With that, he shook his head in amazement. After talking with us for some time, he told me that he was charging me for breaking and entering and that I would do prison time even if I elected a jury trial.

To my amazement, and why I love this coach to this day, he stood up and said, "Well, if that is what you have planned for Patrick, I guess I have no other choice then but to go to the press and let them know your son was having an illegal marijuana party."

With that, the judge actually got silent. Then he said, "Patrick, you and your partner are going to do one hundred community hours, and, Coach, I have always taken care of your players when they have gotten into some trouble. Now I will let you know that because I am not convicting any of these young men and giving them community service while in my chambers, be aware that this is the last time I will be easy on any of your players." With that, we walked out of his courtroom, and the coach never brought it up again, not that I am aware of.

All my friends also learned that I used the expression BA, and I never really had a meaning for it. It's funny because just recently a good friend told me it really used to piss her off when I said BA. I asked her why, and she always thought it meant *bad ass*, and we both started laughing in our texts. Another crazy time was a friend of mine, Jerry, went four wheeling in the hills above his house that was a mansion on the Kern River. His dad was one of the biggest or was the biggest home builder in Bakersfield. Well, our four wheeling did not consist of four-wheel vehicles. It involved his Ford pickup that got stuck halfway up the hill. So then he took his sister's sedan to tow his truck off the hill, but it also got stuck on the hill. So there were two cars stuck in the hill, and to this day, I don't remember how they got them down.

When Mike was a junior and senior, I got to be friends with some of his friends who were a year older than him. One of them that I spent a lot of time with was Mike.

When I dropped out of college, I got a job in construction working as a plumber on a new construction site. I always seemed to be attracted to construction jobs, and so this opportunity was a great one for me. By this time, I wasn't getting along with my dad, and eventually one day I found all my clothes on the front lawn! I think he was telling me it was time to move out. So fortunately, Dave, who was a year older than Mike and went to high school with him, had gotten the same eviction notice from his dad. So it was perfect we found an apartment and moved in together in a furnished two-bedroom apartment. Living with Dave was one of my favorite times in my life, because it was so crazy. We really hit it off as friends from the very beginning and would become lifetime best friends. He had been going to college and working at the same time. He started working construction and doing concrete work when he was around sixteen years old. By the time I moved in with him, he had built up a good business. It was funny because he was five years younger than me, but much more responsible than I was. No kidding! Within a month, I was calling him "son," and he was calling me "pops," but because he was responsible, it should have been the other way around.

It seemed like we would have a party at our apartment every weekend, even if it was only five or six friends. Dave also loved to hunt and was very good at it. During deer season, he would kill enough deer that the venison would last us almost till the next season. He also would go to the Channel Islands and would kill wild boar, and many times he would deep-pit BBQ, and it was delicious. He also would even hunt rabbits and make rabbit stew, which I didn't like. Fortunately for me, every time I needed a job, Dave would hire me. Well, one time when we were finishing flatwork, it started getting real hot (Bakersfield could top 115 on real hot days), so we were working our butts off that the concrete didn't go on us. I didn't pay attention, but I got up for a small rest and some water. Dave said, "Pat, take off your kneepads," and when I did, my jeans were soaked with blood. So I took my jeans off to my ankles, and my knees where swelled up and looked like I had burns with concrete in them. I went to the emergency room and found out I had cement poisoning in both knees. The next day I went to the doctor, and he put me on different medicines, including a type of steroid. Even though I told him I was allergic to steroids, he still gave them to me. Within a few days, not only did my knees get more infected, but my stomach started to bleed. The work comp said this was not work related, so I had to go to the VA in Los Angeles because I didn't have medical insurance.

They found I had a bad staph infection in both knees, so they isolated me in a room by myself that had no window that I could look out and no TV. Luckily my fiancée brought me a small portable TV. I had it for a day, and the VA had the workers check to make sure it was compliant with them and found it wasn't, so now I had no TV and would be stuck in that little room for a month, until the staph infection cleared.

Thank God my fiancée's dad was the senior partner of a large firm in Bakersfield and also had offices in LA, and he referred me to an attorney who specialized in work comp cases. He not only got me a great settlement from the work comp, because they said it was not work related, but also sued the doctor who treated me for negligence in giving me steroids knowing that I was allergic to them. Even though this doctor's staff falsified their records, he proved that they indeed gave them to me, and so I was awarded a good amount of money. Another thing I was awarded was for work comp to pay for my education to be trained in another field. So I chose a private college to train to be a computer programmer and analysis, which I completed.

My first job offer was with a solar company located in the Tehachapi Mountains, and I took it. I was programming a mainframe to keep track of how much energy was lost due to the wind being too high and the turbines automatically shutting down when the wind hit a certain level. For example, maybe when the wind grew to 40 mph, the turbines would automatically turn off. At this time, I didn't have a car, so I went looking for a car to buy. I found a perfect car, and I bought it, but the problem with this sale was that I was drunk when I bought it, and it was very dark, so I could not even make out the color. The next morning I woke up and looked at the car I bought the night before. I had an idea I made a mistake, when the first thing that caught my eye about this old Mustang was the color of the car was faded and was an ugly yellow. The next thing I noticed when I took a look inside was that the turn signal level was being held by a woman's hair band.

Going up the Tehachapi Mountains in the summer was hot, even at the summit of the mountain where the Zond headquarters were located. I was really upset the first day of my job. I drove up to Zond and found out the air-conditioning did not work. Well, all that summer I was so crazy with having to look good, I would drive up there with all my windows closed so people passing me would think I had AC. It's funny looking back at it that by the time I arrived to my job, I was soaking wet from all my sweat, but people passing me would not notice that. Ha-ha. Also, probably before I had been working there for a month, all of these guys in my department were smart and graduated from schools like Cal Berkeley majoring in computer science. They would look at me and laugh and say, "How the hell did you get into this profession? You have a personality."

Another friend who was a year older than my brother was Mike M., and we became very good friends because he got me a job with his dad's company APW (Auto Parts Warehouse), which was the biggest auto parts warehouse in Kern County. His grandpa had started a chain of auto parts stores called Southern Auto, and they also dominated Kern County before all the chain auto parts stores had even started. His dad was always great to me and would sometimes have to call me in his office, not so much that I wasn't a good worker, but just to try to straighten me out from being so crazy, especially when I drank. His mom and dad were very young and sometimes would get together with the parents of Buzz, another good friend who was a year older than my brother, and I would party with the parents. I was old enough that I could have been his parents' younger brother. So I really got close to his mom and dad, and they were always trying to get me to drink more in moderation so I wouldn't get crazy. Mike and I had some great times, especially he would invite me to their cabin at Bass Lake during the Fourth of July, and they had a speed boat that probably could have raced in professional races.

One time when he was towing me behind the boat, while I was on a big inner tube, he turned the boat around, and I went flipping in the water, and when I surfaced, he thought he really hurt me, because my face was full of blood. With my nose, it didn't take much for it to bleed like a shive. Another time I will never forget is we used to go up the canyon, a small two-lane curvy road that led to Lake Isabella and on into Kernville, and stop somewhere along the way and party. Well, we were getting back into his big 4x4, and he started to take off without me. He didn't realize it, but he ran over my foot. I was in so much pain yelling at him that he had run over my foot, but he and everyone in the truck thought I was joking around and were laughing their heads off. Finally they stopped laughing because they saw I was in pain, and I yelled, "My shoe is filling up with blood!" So I took off my shoe. There was no blood, and then they were laughing so hard they couldn't stop. They were saying, "Rat, you're so drunk, you wouldn't know if Mike ran you over." With that, I took off my sock, and they saw my foot was about twice the size it should be, and they rushed me to the ER.

I was notorious that when I got in an ER, which was too often, I thought all the nurses wanted me! So as my usual self, I was hopping around trying to get one of the nurses to get on the bed with me. Since my dad was a hospital administrator, they would always call my dad and let him know what was going on. As soon as he started yelling at me, I realized I better settle down. They took x-rays, and the bones in my foot were broken, so they put me in a temporary cast since my foot was so swollen and would wait a few days to put a permanent cast on after the swelling went down. Mike really did feel bad. There was a truck-stop place that we would always go to after a late night of drinking, so he and his friends said they would buy me a big breakfast. We all ate, and I thought we were ready to go, but Mike and our friends said they had to use the restroom. The next thing I knew, I heard loud honking; and there they were in the truck again laughing their heads off, because they knew I had no money (Mike always paid for me.) They were dining and dashing (not paying). So off I went with my crutches hobbling as fast as I could out the front door while one of the waitresses was yelling and trying to catch me. Thank God I made it to the truck with a few friends carrying me, and we took off without paying.

Another funny story is when a couple of friends of mine decided to drive to Pismo Beach in a new small Toyota pickup with a shell. They both liked to smoke pot, and I liked to drink, so they were in the back of the truck, and I sat in front with my six-pack of beer. The back window slid open so we could talk, but I kept it closed most of the way because I didn't want the pot smoke to get into the cab. The route we took was through land that was all agricultural, on a little two-lane road. After about an hour, they were pretty high, and I probably had already drunk at least three beers. I started to get a little worried because I had no idea where we were. So I slid open the back window and said, "I think we are lost. I have no idea where we are." With that, they just started cracking up, and I said, "What the hell is so funny?"

In return, they said, "Rat, don't worry, just keep driving. The truck will drive itself to the beach." (This was way before GPS or cell phones for that matter). I opened up another can of beer and said to myself, *Okay, Truck, if I get too drunk, you just go ahead and take us to the beach.* I finished the six-pack, and they probably finished an ounce of pot (just kidding), and somehow we got to the beach. The first thing we did was rent horses so we could ride along the beach. I led the way, and we had to follow the trail that led to the beach, which part of the way was next to a cliff with the beach beyond. I do not like heights, and so I was a little freaked out, especially after drinking a six-pack, although looking down over the cliff sort of sobered me up. If you know my friends who were high, the rest of the story should not surprise me. They also liked to smoke cigarettes, so you guessed it, they decided to put the burnt end of one of their cigarettes on the ass of my horse. I had no idea what they did. All I know is that my horse went friggin' crazy, and I thought it was the end of my life, because to me, the horse just wanted to buck me off and throw me over the cliff. This went on for a half hour. No, I'm exaggerating. It probably lasted five minutes at the most, and my horse settled down. They caught up with me and could barely stay on their horses because they laughed so hard. It was hard for them to tell me why the horse went crazy. I think this was the last time I drove to the coast with them, and I believe one of them drove us home, because I bought a few more beers at the beach, and I think I was pretty much passed out by the time we got in the truck to go back home.

The next story is probably one of the most important chapters because it had a major life-changing impact on my life.

When I was around twenty-seven, the movie *Saturday Night Fever* had come out with John Travolta, which started the craze of disco and disco music. Even in Bakersfield, a club opened featuring disco.

As I was always having an identity crisis, way back in high school, I didn't know if I should be a jock or a hippie, although I never really was going to be a hippie living with my dad having had a military career, because if you were considered a hippie, you were a peace freak against the Vietnam War. I decided maybe the way to attract women was to become a disco dud. So off I went and bought my disco outfit and was ready to go to the club that Friday night. Well, I got there and actually felt uncomfortable wearing these weird clothes trying to look like John Travolta. As soon as I walked in, typical Bakersfield, there were a few guys not dressed in their disco uniforms but dressed like normal Bakersfield guys with blue jeans, big buckle on their belt, and cowboy hats. All of a sudden, I thought I would look better as a cowboy. So when I had had a few drinks and was ready to ask this one lady for a dance, I asked one of the guys if I could wear his cowboy hat. I thought that way if she liked cowboys better than disco duds, I had a better chance of her saying yes if I asked her to dance. Can you imagine how I looked all decked out in my disco outfit with a cowboy hat! I'm sure I stood out, and maybe that is why she said yes, because she wanted to find out what the hell was up with this guy.

After the dance, I gave my hat back to one of the guys, and this lady and I got a table and had a few drinks and danced the rest of the night. About one hour before they closed, she told me she had to leave to go to work. I said, "Wow, what kind of work do you do that starts at two in the morning?" Well, she and a few friends cleaned the club after it closed. I thought, *This is where I find out if she is interested in me.* So I asked her if she needed help.

She said, "Are you serious you would help us?"

I said, "Of course, and you do not have to pay me." It turned out one of the girls who helped her wasn't there, so she was really glad that I would help her. That was the beginning of a three- to six-month relationship. We started going out, and many Fridays and Saturdays, I would help clean the club, and she would come over to my apartment afterward to have some extracurricular activity. The problem with this relationship from the beginning was that she had a five- or six-year-old boy, and even though she was getting divorced, she still lived with her husband. It turned out her husband was the Mr. Travolta of Bakersfield and would dance on the stage or in front of the stage. He also was a black belt in karate. I may be dumb, but I'm not stupid, and even though I liked to fight, I stayed away from him the whole time I was taking out his wife. At the time, he had no idea I was seeing his wife, and we would be at the club when he was there. Many times we would be drinking at one of the tables in the back and making out, while he was trying to impress the women with his disco moves. This girl was a fox; and I started thinking for the first time that I might want to ask her to marry me, that is, when she divorced her husband.

The relationship was going great, and then she found out how much I liked to drink, and she did not know if I would be a Dr. Jekyll or Mr. Hyde from one night to the other. The beginning of the end was one day she had asked me to pick up her son and bring him home. Her husband now knew I was the boyfriend. Well, as usual, I had a few beers before I picked him up, and she came to the driver's side to give me a kiss and smelled the beer, and shit hit the fan. "What the hell are you doing driving with my son while you've been drinking?" Needless to say, I didn't have an answer, and things got progressively worse to the point that she wasn't spending as much time with me. So after a while, I figured she must be seeing someone else, and I also was not helping her clean anymore after the club closed.

So one Saturday I decided I was going to follow her to see where she was going. The next thing I knew, I saw red flashing lights behind me, so I pulled over, and the police had me get out of the car and do a field sobriety test. I was smashed as usual, so they began to put handcuffs on me. It turned out I was not following her, but she was following me and pulled over to see what was going to happen. I guess I was yelling loud enough for her and a girlfriend to hear. I told the officers to take off their guns and we would find out how tough they were. Well, they didn't obey my commands but proceeded to knock me out by slamming my head against their car. The next thing

I knew, I was in the booking area of the jail with a bunch of officers nearby.

According to the police report, I had some more words to tell them, and I said, "You guys are real tough. Why don't you take those badges off and we will see how tough you really are?" Well, they didn't obey my commands either but took me to a secluded padded cell and proceeded to beat the hell out of me, until once again I was knocked out.

When my dad came to bail me out, he looked at me and said, "My god, someone beat the hell out of you."

When we got to the car, I told him, "Dad, I wasn't in a fight. The police did this to me." He was on the way to take me to the emergency room anyway, but he made sure that they took pictures of me. I was diagnosed with a concussion, a broken nose, several broken ribs, and huge bruises from my wrists all the way up to my shoulders. My dad was livid and said, "They are not getting away with this. I don't care what you said to them." My dad being a hospital administrator had a lot of respect in the town and was good friends with a few of the local judges, so he made an appointment for us to see one of them. My dad brought all the pictures, and I proceeded to tell the judge what I could remember happened and also let him know what my girlfriend had seen.

After listening and reviewing the pictures, he told my dad that hell yes, we had a great case against the police department, and he knew a few good lawyers who would take our case. But before we left, he said, "Remember, Frank, this is not Orange County where you used to live. This is a small city and has a much different mind-set than larger cities." He proceeded to say, "I really think you have a good case, but like I said, this is a small town, and due to that fact, they will do everything in their power to make Patrick's life miserable. In fact, if you proceed, I suggest Pat move back down south, and even then, you and your family will not want to break any kind of law, even a traffic ticket."

Well, we got home and talked with my mom who by the way was more upset with what happened to me ("Another concussion! How many can he take?") than my dad. So we decided to not proceed with a lawsuit, and I would keep my mouth closed if ever pulled over again. And to this day, if I get pulled over, my hands go on the steering wheel, and all I say is "Yes, sir or ma'am" or "No, sir or ma'am." And after that incident, I have had nothing but respect for every kind of police officer.

The reason this story is so important is I was devastated by my breakup with this woman. Not only was she the cutest lady I had gone out with, but I really did love her. I could not imagine living without her, and I didn't know what to do except I had to get out of town. So I decided to enlist in the navy at the age of twenty-eight, and that sure would keep me from stalking her. Sometime during this period of my life, I got into a fight at a bar and would actually win according to my friends; but once again I would go to the doctor to find I had shattered my orbital bone, which I think is around your eye. Lucky for me, they couldn't put that in a cast! Ha-ha.

6

Navy

I made the decision to enlist in the navy, so before I actually signed up, they had me take a few tests to see where I might best fit in with regard to what I would do. A few days later, I went back to the recruiting office, and the guys were very excited. They said, "Patrick, not very many recruits qualify for this, but you qualify to go to school to become a naval journalist." They said, "As an enlisted man, this is considered one of the best jobs you can have." I enlisted and started boot camp in San Diego sometime in October of 1978. When I arrived and was assigned to a company, I was much older than the rest of the recruits. Most of them were just out of high school, and I was twenty-eight years old. The company commanders for some reason liked me from the start, maybe because I was older and still willing to join the navy. I also started with the rank of E3, while most or all the recruits started as an E1 or E2, but I had some college, so that helped me to start as an E3. The commanders made me the yeoman of our company, which basically is the secretary.

I hadn't been in boot camp for two weeks when I got very sick with pneumonia and was in the hospital for seven to ten days, with very high fever, to the point they had to wrap me in ice to get my fever to go down. When I got out and returned to my company, I was still very weak, so my commanders had me do very little. No one was supposed to be in the barracks when we were doing any exercises like learning about ships, fire integrity, etc. But I was so weak my commanders would have me take my blanket and pillow from my bunk and lay it under the bunk and sleep while the rest of the company was doing drills. As I said, the commanders, who were both senior chiefs, really liked me; and on a few occasions, they had me over at their living quarters and would let me drink a beer or two with them and then go back to my barracks. So for me, boot camp was a cake walk, especially the physical conditioning, because it was so easy. It was amazing, however, how many of these young men were so out of shape they could not complete a mile run without resting.

When graduation came, my dad showed up, along with my brother Mike and his girlfriend. Once it was finished, I was officially on leave for two weeks; so my brother, knowing me, knew the first thing I wanted to do was go out drinking. Somehow the idea of going to Tijuana, Mexico, came up; so he and his girlfriend along with Buzz, his roommate, crossed the border to Mexico. Mike was living in San Diego and playing football for San Diego State, along with his roommate Buzz. Somehow the topic of going to a "donkey show" came up, so we wound up going, along with his poor girlfriend. I don't think this show particular drew a lot of women to them.

I believe I stayed in San Diego for a night or two and then went up to Bakersfield where I stayed with my dad, until I had to leave to go to my A school. I was in Bakersfield for the rest of my leave; and while there, a day or two before I had to head to Indianapolis, Indiana, where my school was located, I was helping my son, Dave, pour some concrete. He didn't notice, but I was in the trenches, helping move the concrete from the truck into the foundation. When he saw me, he yelled, "Rat, what the hell are you doing! You're damn near up to your knees in concrete, without boots on. Get the hell out of there before you get hurt!" Well, the damage had already been done. I took off my shoes and socks, and I had serious concrete burns on both feet. Thank God I was not officially employed with him, so it would not be another work comp case. When I went to the doctor, they took care of my feet and told me not to wear any kind of socks or shoes, until they healed. The problem was that I was taking a flight the next morning to Indianapolis and had to report in my full uniform. This meant I had to wear black socks along with hard dress shoes.

When we arrived at the airport in Indianapolis, my feet were so swollen I could not even walk, so they had to carry me to a wheelchair where they lifted me into the transport van. Instead of going directly to my barracks, they took me to the base hospital. The doctors had to cut my shoes off me, and then after putting all kinds of stuff on my feet to soften up the socks (they had dried up and had puss all over them), they proceeded to rip the socks off, not too comfortable by any means. Thankfully they did give me some pain medication to help with the pain. So due to this condition, I did not have to wear any kind of shoes for around the first six to eight weeks of school to let my feet heal. When I had left San Diego Airport, the temperature was around seventy degrees, which I was used to. When I arrived in Indianapolis, the temperature was negative twenty degrees with the windchill factor. I remember thinking, *What the hell have I got myself into this time?*

When I arrived, it was during the Christmas holidays, so there were very few people in the barracks because the school was closed for a week for the holidays. But as luck would have it, I found a guy who turned out to be a great friend during school, and he was from San Diego. He had been in the navy for four or six years and finally qualified for the journalism school. The barracks had a basement that was called the dayroom, with a pool table and other games. But the best part that we liked the most was that it had a Coke machine, but instead of soda drinks, it was full of beer. It so happened that Skip liked to drink also, so by the time the week was over, the machine was empty. One night we decided to go off base to a nearby club to have a few drinks. Well, we decided between the two of us, we had enough money for each of us having one more drink or leaving and paying for a cab. What the hell, we were not even a mile from the base, so you know what option we chose. However, these two California boys forgot we were in Indianapolis; and when we left the bar, I believe is was minus fifteen degrees. By the time we had maybe walked a few blocks, we both were freezing cold. Someone who had also been at the bar saw us and pulled over and took us to the base. The first thing he said was "What the hell are you guys thinking? You could have gotten severe frostbite." And in addition, I still had bad feet but had put some kind of soft boots on, but it still hurt like hell to walk.

He then said, "You guys aren't from around here evidently," and we both said no, we just came from California. He shook his head and said something like "Figures. A couple of crazy California boys."

Once school started, I really loved it; and my roommate was a kid, around twenty-one, who was in the marines. The journalism school was multiservice, which meant it consisted of all the branches of the service, including navy, marines, army, and air force. We had it made compared to other A schools, because we actually got separate rooms for two men. Most A schools, you would be with everyone in a large barrack. I had been in the school for probably two months when things started going a little sour. I was great friends with the sergeant who was in charge of us, and under him was our commanding officer, a young woman who was a lieutenant in the navy.

I started drinking more than I should have on the weekends, including Sunday nights. Like I said, I really liked the sergeant, but one morning I had been up all night throwing up, and it looked like I was throwing up blood, but I was too drunk to care. It got time for us all to get up, with morning call, but I could not get up. I felt so bad with a hangover. By the time everyone was dressed and most of them were already outside in formation, I was still in my bunk, lying on my side facing the wall. The sergeant walked in and called my name and rank and said who he was along with his rank, and he told me, "Get out of your bunk right now, and this is a direct order!"

I told him, "Sorry, Sarge, I can't do it." I believe they said he tried to get me up several times, and I still wouldn't get up. The next thing I knew, some woman was yelling at me. "Patrick McNeese"— with my rank and everything else—"this is Lieutenant Fuzzy, and this is a direct order! Get out of your bunk now or you will be arrested!" I was still facing the wall, so I really didn't know if it was the lieutenant or friends trying to pull a joke on me. And I responded with "I don't care if you are a fleet admiral. I'm not getting up for anyone." With that, the MPs dragged me out of bed and began to drag me down the hallway to the squad car. Fortunately for me, right in front of the lieutenant's office, I began to throw up violently; and I guess they said it was mostly blood. So instead of going to the base jail, I was going to a nearby hospital. I was there for around a week, when the doctors decided they wanted to do exploratory surgery to find out where the bleeding was coming from. However, before I consented, a few officers from the navy came in and said, "We are not authorizing for any operation, and we are transferring you to a military hospital."

I didn't have a choice, so they medevaced me by a small plane with a few medics to an air force base hospital in Ohio. I was in the hospital for around two weeks, and the bleeding stopped, but they were not able to actually determine where the source of the bleeding was coming from, but they did tell me to slow down on my drinking. The day I was released, I found out that everyone in the school was waiting for my return. Not because they missed me, but that I had been charged with a general court-martial, and they wanted to see what was going to happen. I had no idea that the lieutenant had filled out the paperwork for a court-martial, and so when I got back to the base, I just thought everything was going to return to normal. But when I got back to school, the sergeant met me and said the lieutenant wanted to see me right away. I went into her office, and she asked that I close the door. The first thing she said was "Mr. McNeese, I'm glad to see you back, because with all the blood you lost, we did not know if we would ever see you again. Now to more important matters. Do you recall anything that happened that morning?"

I said, "I remember not getting out of my bunk when you ordered me to."

She said, "And do you remember what you told me?"

I said, "No, not really."

"Well, let me read to you what you said to me word by word that I have written in this document in front of me. You said, and I quote, 'I don't give a damn if you're a friggin' fleet admiral. I'm not getting up for anyone.' Mr. McNeese, do you know how serious it is to disobey a direct command from your commanding officer?"

"Ma'am, I have no excuse for my behavior, and I guess I will have to pay the price for not only disobeying your command, but not respecting you as an officer and as a woman."

"These papers in front of me, Mr. McNeese, are charges for a general court-martial that I filled out; and I only need to send them up the chain of command and your life in the military is going to change dramatically."

I was scared, but I also knew she was serious, and I had no idea what my future was, except I knew I was going to the brig. She then looked at me and said, "Because of your overall condition and mental state and talking to the sergeant, we agreed that we feel you definitely were not in your right mind that morning. And with that..." She began to tear up the papers, and I began to cry like a baby. She proceeded to say, "We feel that you will greatly contribute to the navy, and therefore, I'm not carrying out this court-martial."

I stood up and saluted her and said, "Ma'am, I will prove to you that I will be empowered in everything I do from here on out, and I will not let you down." With that, I walked out of the room.

The sergeant saluted me and said, "Keep up the good work." Because of this incident, I pretty much stopped drinking, which is amazing in itself, and did very well in school. The school consisted of classes for print journalism, classes for photography, and classes for broadcast journalism. I really excelled in broadcasting and was one of the very few who passed the voice requirement needed to potentially be a news broadcaster for AFRTS (Armed Forces Radio and Television Service). I actually won an award for best director for a short feature, which was very significant. The problem was that even though I was not drinking, I would find myself in extreme pain and throwing up blood.

Around three months before I was to graduate, I got orders to be stationed at Clark Air Force Base in the Philippines, along with my friend Skip, who was my good friend from San Diego. Since he had already been in the navy for some time, he told me, "Pat, this is probably the best assignment any journalist could receive. First, we are at an air force base, which means we will get assigned a room, with only one other person; and in all probability since we are going at the same time, it's likely that we will be roommates. And secondly, the Filipino women love military men, and they are beautiful." He had been there previously aboard a ship that had been docked at

Subic Bay Naval Station. I was really excited, but then a few weeks later, I was transported to Great Lakes Naval Hospital, because I was bleeding again. This hospital I guess was one of the largest naval hospitals, and I guess during the Vietnam War, it was filled. But now the hospital was almost deserted, with very few patients. I was there for around two weeks, and once again the bleeding stopped, but they could not find the cause. I went back to the school and would now be behind the current class I was taking, which I believe was photography, so I had to wait until the next class started, maybe a week or two. But it meant that my orders to Clark Air Force Base had been canceled, and I would be getting new orders.

So I started photojournalism again, and this was the last part of the journalism I would have to complete. I really like photography, also, because we not only learned how to take pictures, but also learned how to develop the film and create some of the effects that we desired. I had received new orders by this time, and I was going to be stationed on Midway Island, a small remote island in the South Pacific. I was somewhat disappointed because I was no longer going to be stationed with my friend in the Philippines. Once again I started bleeding and was sent to Great Lakes. This time it seemed like they really didn't care if I lived or died and was on this large ward with maybe one or two other people. It seemed like they only came by to ease my pain, and I don't remember them doing any more tests. So eventually once again the bleeding stopped, and I was sent back to the school. Well, once again my orders had been canceled, but this time the commanding officer of the entire journalism school called me into his office. He had me sit down, and from the beginning, I knew he was a very nice man. He began by saying, "Mr. McNeese, how are you feeling?"

I said, "Physically I'm feeling much better, but I'm getting emotionally distraught because they never can find out what is wrong with me, and this last time I was in the hospital, it didn't seem like they were even trying to find out, sir."

With that, he said, "You know, I really don't know how you have put up with this for the past year. And because I'm also frustrated, I'm going to do something that I'm not supposed to do. When a soldier is sick, he is not supposed to be assigned to another assignment until he is well enough. Well, I'm convinced if you stay here, number 1, you may never leave, and number 2, my biggest concern is that you could die before they even find out what is wrong with you. So what I'm going to do is I'm giving you orders to be assigned to a guided missile cruiser that's home port is San Diego. This ship is not set to sail for a Westpac for another six months, and that is one of the reasons I'm assigning you to her. Due to your history of getting sick every two to three months, I think you will wind up in the naval hospital in San Diego before you set sail."

Within a week, I was flying to San Diego and was aboard the USS *Fox*. My assignment was to be in charge of the SITE system, which was in a huge disarray because they had not had a journalist assigned to the ship I guess for over a year. The first thing I realized was the captain of the ship, for some reason, really liked me and told me that if I needed anything to get the SITE system up and running, I didn't have to go up the chain of command. He had let it be known that I could go directly to him. Once I got on the ship and started getting the SITE system up and running, I was really excited, and it was amazing because so was the crew on the ship. One of the first things I got going was the ship's radio system, and the first time I started playing some records, the captain told me that it had a big effect on the crew. Guys were coming up to me and letting me know how much they appreciated what I was doing, and that just made me more eager to work even harder to get everything in order. I really enjoyed this assignment, and I thought, *Wow, this is even better than being stationed in the Philippines because I'm in charge of everything, and everyone is already happy with what I've already accomplished.*

The ship had not actually been out to sea in quite a while because it was in dry dock, and we were finally going to go out approximately three hundred miles of the coast of California. Since I had been to Catalina numerous times as a kid, I figured this would not be a big deal, like it was for some of the crew who had never been out to sea, even in a private boat. The first time we went out to sea was to show our flag to Mexico, so we made several port stops to various ports in Mexico. They all appeared to be tourist destinations because of all the

Americans we saw at the ports. This was one of the best memories I have while I was in the navy. The captain was scheduled to be upped from a captain to an admiral, and I was doing a feature story on him for the *Navy Times*. This was perfect because he let me go wherever he went, and he liked to go to restaurants with bars. Actually I don't know if Mexico has a restaurant without a bar at least at tourist destinations. I wasn't allowed to drink, but I really enjoyed his stories, and me being an enlisted man, this rarely occurred because enlisted men were not to fraternize with officers. I felt almost like he was an uncle because I was getting close to him.

One of the stories he told me, he did not want to be known, so I promised him it would just be between him and me. By that time, he had had several drinks, so I think he felt comfortable telling me. He went on to tell me that one of the reasons the navy delayed in promoting him to admiral was for several years, his girlfriend in San Diego was a professional dancer. Not the kind who did ballet, but the kind who danced around a pole naked. I guess his peers did not think that was such a good idea even for a captain, let alone one who they were considering for a promotion to admiral. He said they really were in love, and he was willing to never make admiral, if it meant breaking up with her. I don't know what happened, but I guess they broke up, and it had been several years since he had been with her, so his name came back up for the promotion.

I believe we were scheduled to be out to sea for five or seven days and then return to San Diego Harbor. Well, we set sail one morning, and everything was going smoothly. Then we got a notice that a big storm was approaching, so we started doing a lot of drills for heavy seas. The storm produced huge seas. The captain, in all his years sailing, had never experienced such large seas, so large that the waves were crashing against the bridge and some over the bridge of the ship. Because of this, a lot of the guys who had never even been on a boat began to get seasick, which is a god-awful condition I guess because I had never experienced it. I was having no problem until I went to the mess hall and began to eat. Before I knew it, a couple of guys were throwing up all over the table, which made me sicker than a dog. I had never experienced the uncontrollable vomiting that I was doing. I tried lying down in my bunk, but that made it worse. The captain heard that I was really sick, so he had a few guys bring me up to the bridge. He told me to go outside on the deck and get some fresh air, and that would make me feel much better. Within thirty minutes, I was no longer sick and felt 100 percent better.

For some reason, this seasickness caused me to not be able to urinate, the same way it had affected me when I was in my A school. So they brought me to sick bay and tried everything they had to relax me so I could urinate, but nothing was working, and the medic on board, not a doctor, was getting worried that if I didn't go to the bathroom soon, there was a good chance that my bladder would tear, which would infect my whole body. I guess he was afraid if that happened, I would not survive. The captain found out and came down to the sick bay to see how I was doing. He told me normally they would call in a helicopter and medevac me to the hospital. But he said that was not possible with the high seas, so he turned the ship back toward the harbor, hoping and praying we would get there before my condition got worse.

Thank God the chaplain also came down to pray with me, but also, he was trained in hypnosis and told the captain if he could get me hypnotized, there was a good chance that I would relax and go to the bathroom. Thank God he said I turned out to be a good subject, and within fifteen or twenty minutes, I was pissing like a racehorse. When we got back to port, the captain could not believe that they had assigned me to a ship, with my known medical conditions. For some reason, this set off me bleeding again, and I was medevaced to the naval hospital in San Diego. I wasn't there for more than two days, when they decided they were going to do exploratory surgery to finally find out where the bleeding was coming from. It was ironic to me because a year earlier, the doctors in a private hospital in Indianapolis wanted to do the same thing, but I was transferred to a military hospital. They did the surgery and found out that my gallbladder was so diseased that it was not even functioning, and that was where the bleeding was coming from. So they removed my gallbladder, and I woke up minus my gallbladder.

After the surgery, I was placed in a large ward with other men, and there were only curtains for each bed to provide privacy. I was in the hospital for around seven to ten days to recover, because they basically cut me in half due to the fact that they didn't know where the bleeding was coming from, so they had to make a big-enough incision to be able to look at all my organs. Around two or three days after the surgery, I was still in a lot of discomfort, but I kept noticing the doctors attending to the guy who was in a bed directly in front of me. One morning, all hell broke loose; it seemed like there were more doctors and nurses attending to this guy than were on the entire ward. They didn't close the curtains, so I saw everything that was transpiring. The next thing I saw was they were putting paddles on this guy, and his whole body seemed to be jumping off the bed. It seemed like it went on for a half hour, but it was so dramatic for me, it could have only been fifteen minutes. Then all of a sudden, everyone started leaving except for a couple of nurses and a doctor. When I saw them put a sheet over his head, I knew he must have died. I had never seen anyone die, so I was like shaking in my bed, thinking, *Oh my god, if he died, what about me? I'm going to be next.*

The doctor looked over at me, and maybe I was a little pale, because he came over and said, "Pat, I'm so sorry you had to see this. We didn't even have time to pull the curtains." Then he said, "When was the last time you had some pain medication?" He said, "Wait, here is your chart. Let me look." Then he said, "Good. You haven't had any for four hours. To help you calm down, I'm going to add a type of medication with it that will help settle you down." I don't know what he gave me, but an hour later, I really didn't care if everyone on the ward died, including him and the nurses, so I guess it worked.

When I got discharged, I was temporarily assigned to the base public relations department, because I needed to get new orders, and specifically not be assigned to a ship unless it was an aircraft carrier that had a hospital. By this time, I not only wanted to do my four years, I wanted to make a career with the navy. Well, that plan didn't go the way I wanted it to, because evidently the navy was tired of me constantly visiting the hospital. So I might have been at the public relations department for a week, when a couple of officers met with me and told me that the navy actually wanted to discharge me early. They convinced me that I would get a certain percentage of pay for the rest of my life and that I would get a pretty good amount of money the day I signed the discharge papers. They really were telling me I didn't have a choice, so I agreed with them and maybe a week later was no longer in the navy.

My brother was still going to school at San Diego State, and there were a few guys he had lived with who still were renting a house near the college, so they let me move in with them and pay rent until I could find a place of my own, which was perfect. Even after everything I went through, I was really depressed because I wanted to stay in the navy; and now at the age of thirty-one, what was I going to do when I grew up? So I started drinking heavily again. I found a bar that I really liked that was close to the navy port in San Diego, so I started going there, and on weekends, they had a live band.

After a month or so, it seemed like it was full of women, way more than usual, and not a lot of men. That's when I was told by a guy in the navy that a carrier group had just left on a Westpac, and a lot of the wives were looking for temporary boyfriends. He went on to say, "You have never heard the nickname for this place." I said no. He said, "This place is known as the Westpac Widows, because all their husbands are going to be gone for at least nine months to a year, and they need to find a boyfriend."

With that, I started looking for a potential girlfriend. The next Friday or Saturday, I met a woman, but she was not married to a guy in the navy. She was getting divorced, and this place was just close enough to her house that she and her cousin who also lived nearby would go frequently and not have to be bothered by men trying to pick them up, because they knew they weren't widows! They were Vietnamese, and I became very attracted to Lilly (not her real name). So before I knew it, we began going out. Her mother lived with her and her two sons, and her mom was very traditional, so when I would come to visit especially late at night, if her mom was still awake, you could slice the tension with a knife. I have no idea what they were saying when they were yelling at each other because

I barely spoke English, let alone Vietnamese. It turned out that her cousin told her that since I was temporarily living with a guy in the navy, I could move into her house. This seemed like a great idea, because Lilly didn't have to argue with her mom anymore; she would just tell her she was spending the night with her cousin.

Unbeknownst to me, the cousin's brother was a secretary for the Hasson's bike club. All I knew was he seemed like a very good guy, and we would drink beer together. Also, her cousin's boyfriend was a welder working for the navy, and he lived there also but was not a biker. We actually all got along great. I didn't have transportation. I had been using my brother's Silver Streak, an old 240z that was on its last leg. Bill, the welder, had a Yamaha 300, and he sold it to me for a good price, but he said, "The first thing you have to do is buy a new rear tire because it is bald."

I had really never ridden a motorcycle, so he actually gave me lessons, and by the time I was ready to really ride, I felt comfortable and confident. On occasion, her brother would have over a group of the bikers, and we would all be drinking beer, and they would get on me and say, "Pat, you and that rice burner of yours would not even make a prospect in this club," and then laugh their asses off.

One weekend the chapter of the hessians that her brother belonged to was all getting together for a ride to a known biker bar around twenty miles from where we lived. I was totally surprised when they invited me to ride with them. I think they were all going to get a laugh with this crazy guy on his Yamaha 300. They all had their biker uniforms, but my uniform was generally a tank top with cutoff jeans and flip-flops. So here I went following them. They were all on their Harley-Davidsons while I was on my rice burner. We got on the freeway; and for some reason, maybe because I had already had a few drinks, I decided I was going to show them how fast my rice burner could go. So I might have got up to 80 mph and passed them all and met them in the bar's parking lot. The next thing I knew, Bob, my biker roommate, took me by the scruff of the neck and led me into the restroom. Then he shoved me up against the wall, and he was a strong and husky guy. He said, "What the hell do you think you were doing?"

I said, "Well, you guys always make fun of my Yamaha 300, so I thought I would show you how fast I was going."

He said, "You have no idea what you just did, do you?"

I said, "No, I have no idea."

With that, he said, "It's lucky they aren't in here carving you up with their knives."

I went, "My god, what the hell did I do?"

He said, "You passed the 'leader of the pack,' the president of that chapter." He added, "I wouldn't even ever do that, and I'm third in command."

Thank God the president knew what a crazy person I was, so they laughed about that whole night. I think I got so drunk they called a cab to take me home.

Like I had said previously, the rice burner had a bald rear tire, and a bald rear tire on a motorcycle is not a good idea. After having it a few months, the guy who sold it to me stole it from me and said he wasn't giving it back to me until I got a rear tire. He knew me, and he made decent money, so he paid for a new tire and said, "Pat, I could never live with myself if you killed yourself on that bike because you never got a new tire." I actually had gotten in a small accident he didn't know about. I was taking off with my normal uniform one night to buy a six-pack, and I might have been going 10 mph, but I hit a wet spot on the street I lived on, and the bike came out from under me and landed on top of me. A couple of guys heard the crash; so they lifted the bike off me, looked down at my bare feet, and said, "God, look at your big toe. It's lucky that thing stayed on your foot." I was pretty drunk, and I guess it wasn't that bad because it healed without me having to go to the doctor.

I had been living with Rosie, Lilly's cousin, for a few months; and Lilly and I broke up. I believe it was because she had to choose between me and her mom, and her mom won. That was because sometimes I would sneak over to her house to have some extracurricular activity, and her mom found out and was not too pleased. I was still living with Rosie, but her boyfriend moved out, and an old boyfriend moved in. This boyfriend was not working, so he would sit around watching TV all day drinking. Needless to say, we became good friends, so both of us would drink some whisky (he didn't like beer), and we would watch soap operas all day. He used to give Rosie what he called get go, and whatever it was, we started doing housework at eight in the morning and would still be doing it at two in the afternoon. I'm not sure how many times she would vacuum in one day or clean windows, but she kept busy. Another thing he liked to do was get high on magic mushrooms. I had never tried them, so one evening we all ate some, and I have never laughed so hard in my life. Her boyfriend and I laughed even harder because Rosie had a complete opposite reaction to them. They made her angry, and she was in the front yard, trying to yank out a ten-foot tree. The more she tried, the more frustrated she got, and that caused us to laugh even harder. I didn't know it, but he also did heroin.

I went with him one time when he was picking some up, and we stopped at a laundromat so he could go into the bathroom and shot up. He came back and said, "Have you ever tried this?"

I said, "Hell no." He convinced me to try, and so we went into the bathroom together, and he put a needle in my vein, and in went the heroin. By the time we got back to his car, I was incredibly high, and it was the best feeling I had ever experienced. Within a half hour, I was asking for more, and he said, "No way, I gave you too much, and I'm glad you didn't overdose.

Rosie found out that he had shot me up and was livid. "What the hell are you doing trying to turn Pat into a heroin addict?" I don't know why because I liked the high so much, but that was the first and only time I did heroin.

One night I had gone to a bar and came back home and was in a fighting mood. Someone was sleeping on the couch with his old lady (biker term), and I became very angry yelling at them and telling them to get off my damn couch. Remember I was a roommate, and it wasn't my couch. I was yelling so loud that everyone came out to see what was going on. By that time, I was out of my mind and jumped up and grabbed the ceiling fan that was on in the dining room. I guess it slung me so hard that I went through the dining room window and landed in the front yard. One of the neighbors called the police because they thought there was a huge fight going on. When the police arrived, the bikers were sitting next to me trying to calm me down. I had cut my hands so bad. I was bleeding all over and kept saying, "Oh my god, how many people did I kill?"

They kept telling me no one was hurt and not to worry. The police came and calmed me down so they could take me to the hospital. Luckily I only had to have one finger stitched up. When I got home, everyone was still awake to make sure I was okay. We all went to bed, and when I woke up, they had a talk with me. They said, "Pat, we're sorry, but you're going to have to move out by Monday. We are doing this for your safety, because in normal situations like this, you would not be alive, because one of us would have killed you and thrown your body in the ocean." That was on a Saturday. My room had its own door to get in and out of the house. And I would park my Yamaha 300 in my room. Well, I was really depressed thinking, *My god, I'm getting kicked out by bikers, for god's sake.* So in the moment, my best thinking said, *Okay, God isn't going to let you die from drinking, so the next best thing is to kill yourself.* The easiest and painless way I thought of was to start up the rice burner in my room, and I would die from the exhaust.

Needless to say, I hadn't thought it through very hard because the bike might have been on for fifteen seconds before everyone in the house came into my room saying, "What the hell are you doing now?"

I wasn't going to tell a bunch of hessians that I was trying to kill myself, so I said, "Well, I was bored, and I thought I would tune up my bike."

They looked at each other and started cracking up, saying, "For god's sake, tune it up? You don't even know how to change a spark plug," and with that, I lived to tell this story.

When I moved out, I had no place to go, so I lived on the street in Balboa Park, near the San Diego Zoo. Back then, it wasn't hard to get someone to give you a dollar, and I would use it to buy a cheap bottle of wine. I'm not sure how long I lived there, maybe only a month or two, and I got deathly sick from eating a nut called bitterroot, which came I believe from Guam. I had eaten them before and had no problem, but this time it caused severe food poisoning.

Someone called the police because I was throwing up so bad, and they took me to the VA hospital, where I guess I had such a high fever I was hallucinating and was packed in ice to get my fever down. When I got better, they knew I was crazy, so they threw me in the psych ward, and I was given some Thorazine. I had never had this, but I can tell you that my experience was I would leave my room to get a drink of water, maybe fifty feet away, and the next thing I knew, eight hours later I was getting back to my room.

Before long, they said, "We don't think you're crazy. We think you are just a drunk, so we are transferring you to a program for drunks just like you."

I said, "Will I still be able to take the drug you are giving me?"

They said, "No, this program is intended to get you to stop drinking and everything else that gets you high."

7

Sobriety

When they transferred me, I found out a week earlier a guy jumped off the eighth story and dropped to his death. I guess he didn't like the idea of not drinking anymore. I stayed in the program for a month and had not drank that month, which was the first time of no drinking for that length of time, probably since I was in ninth grade. They transferred me to a halfway house, and I had gotten a sponsor while I was in the program. My sponsor was a great guy, probably at least 6'5" and 230 lbs. and in good shape. He didn't take any shit, and I wasn't going to give him any. He was an ex-con who had turned his life around and had a beautiful wife. They would have me over for dinner, and we would work on a step. We went through all the steps, and he said, "Okay, now it's time for you to start living and move out of the halfway house and get a job."

My best thinking was to tell him, "I think I will move back to Bakersfield, and I know that I can get a job there."

He said, "Wait a minute. You're going to Bakersfield after living in San Diego." He told me, "I believe you are making a huge mistake and setting yourself up to drink again, because from what you have told me, all your friends up there like to drink." But he said, "You have been sober for over four months, and I can't keep you from going, so good luck. Get involved right away with AA so you have a good support system up there."

I moved up to Bakersfield and got a job and moved in with a guy who was the son of a friend that my mom worked with. It was a perfect match. He liked to drink, and I was perfect for him since I didn't drink. I would drive to the nightclubs, he would get drunk, and I would drive us home, without either of us getting a drunk driving. Bill was also taking dancing lessons, so he would set me up sometimes with someone in his class. I found myself not going to AA meetings, not getting a new sponsor, and not reading the Big Book. Before long, I believe the biggest mistake that caused me to drink again was that I was not praying anymore and lost complete contact with God.

One Sunday a bunch of my friends came over to the house. They all liked Bill and were drinking while watching football. They had just come out with wine coolers, and they were drinking those. Before long, I picked one up and took a sip. Before I knew it, all my friends were saying, "What the hell are you doing, Rat? You quit drinking."

I guess I said, "What the hell. This is a wine cooler, like drinking a root beer." Well, I got drunker than hell and was not a happy drunk that night. I guess I slammed my body against a huge tree and then threw myself through the backyard wooden fence. When I woke up the next morning hung over, Bill said, "God, now I know why you don't drink. You're crazy."

I will never forget what I told him. I said, "Bill, you have no idea. The fun has just begun." One Friday I was at a local pizza place, and an old neighbor was with a friend having a pitcher of beer. This neighbor was all grown up and I think was twenty-one, and I was thirty-two. But we hit it off from the beginning and started having extracurricular activities that night since her mom was gone for the weekend. We went out for quite a long time, and I asked her to marry me, and she said yes. The wedding was getting close, and they were just getting ready to have the invitations printed out, and her dad had already paid for our honeymoon in Mexico City. She hated it when I got too drunk but put up with me.

Bill had turned into probably the biggest coke dealer in the valley and was teaching me how to sell it and not use it. One time we went to Vegas to pick up a supply and got there on a Friday night and went to a cathouse before getting to Vegas. I said this because you will see why in a moment. We partied hard that night, and Sunday was the critical day to meet his guy and buy two kilos of coke. He went in and made the deal, and I was outside the car, waiting for him. The keys were in the car, and I had accidentally locked it. When he went to open the door, I thought he was going to pass out because he had two kilos of coke in a big bag and couldn't get in the car. I have never experienced someone unlocking a car with a coat hanger as fast as he did, both of us sweating bullets, not because it was so hot, but because we were so nervous. When we left, he told me, "Okay, this is the toughest part of the drive. If we make it past the border, it is smooth sailing, but before we do, it's going to be nerve-wracking."

We made it back to Bakersfield with no problems, and for some reason, I knew my dad was out of town, so we went to his condo to break the coke up into smaller amounts. I will never forget he was breaking it up with a small hammer on a dining room table and said, "Okay, whatever lands on the floor is yours." You would have thought I was a human vacuum, getting every little bit I could. We finished and went back home. He said, "Okay, the way to make money is not to use this crap, and I'm going to teach you how to break it up and sell it to different kinds of customers, because some like to just snort it, which we mix with filler, and some like to shot it up or freebase it, and that has to be pure coke."

So I started selling it to a few friends, and by this time, my fiancée and I were not having a good relationship. The reason I found the engagement ring on my table is because of this next story. I had sold an ounce to a friend of ours who was a singer and guitar player in a local band that played at one of the top clubs in Bakersfield. One night we went there with some friends to dance and have fun. I got drunk, and I was in a bad mood. This caused me to remember that Ron, the guy in the band, still had not paid me. So when he came over during one of their breaks, I said, "Ron, it's been two weeks, and I still haven't seen any money."

He said, "Don't worry, I will pay you Monday." So he went back onstage and started playing. I got drunker, and the drunker I got, the more pissed I got that I had not been paid. So I decided I was going to get paid then and there. So I hopped on the stage, grabbed a mike, and yelled in it, something like "This jackass has not paid me for the ounce of coke I sold him, and I'm telling him before all of you that he is going to pay me now or I'm going to break his guitar over his head." Before I knew it, the bouncers where trying to get me to leave. With that, I went up the stairs above the dance floor and jumped off to grab a ceiling fan (I guess I like ceiling fans). I came crashing down on to people's tables and breaking a few. The bouncers called the police, and the police came in to arrest me, but I ran as fast as I could through the restaurant, knocking people's food off their tables on my way. I made it to an emergency exit and threw my body into it. The problem was, there was a brick wall waiting for me. When I tried to get up, I realized I could not move. The police came and called an ambulance. When I got to the hospital, I realized I was paralyzed from the neck down. The doctors where scrambling to get x-rays and other tests done. I remember lying there not feeling anything and saying to God, "Okay, you're not going to let me die from this drinking, but this is how I'm going to be for the rest of my life, and I won't be able to drink because I have no use of my arms or anything else to hold a drink."

After they had done all the tests, they found out that nothing was broken; and in all likelihood, I would get all my feeling back once the swelling went down in the discs in my neck. I was in the hospital I think for around a week, and when I got home, I knew the wedding had been called off because the engagement ring was on my table with a note saying something like "I can't live with you because of the way you drink and go crazy." Thank God I started getting my feeling back within a few hours, but it would take over six months for me to recover, and I still have limited motion in my neck. I was seeing the doctor every week, and after around six weeks after being out of the hospital, I saw him, and he didn't like the way I was progressing. I was going to physical therapy just for hot and cold compresses because he didn't want them to work on my neck until the swelling went down. When he saw me, he said, "I don't understand why you are still swollen so badly, and it appears the medicine I'm giving you isn't working."

I said, "Doctor, I will be honest with you. I'm not taking your medicine. I find that a few beers make me more relaxed and work better than any of your pills."

He said, "No wonder the swelling hasn't gone down. When you say a couple of beers each day, how many exactly are you drinking?"

And I told him, "Well, most days I only have a six-pack of beer, but some days I may have more."

He had a look on his face I will never forget, and he said, "A six-pack a day and sometimes more." Then he said, "Have you ever thought that you might have a drinking problem?"

I said, "Of course, especially after this accident when I told God thank you for restoring my feeling, and I will never drink again, and here I am drinking six weeks after I said that."

With that, he told me, "Patrick, there are programs out there that can help you."

I said, "I know. I was in a treatment center in 1982 at VA in San Diego and didn't drink for over a year."

"Well, why don't you go into one up here? What do you have to lose? Because if you keep drinking and not taking my medicines, you could damage your neck much worse than it is now."

When I heard him say those words, I said, "Okay, Doctor, I will check one out." Within a few days, I checked myself into a thirty-day treatment center and have not had a drink since then, which was September of 1985. It was amazing. I was still taking his medicine for swelling and going to physical therapy while in the treatment center, and when I got out thirty days later, almost all the swelling had left my neck, and therapy was actually working on the range of motion on my neck. Sobriety in Bakersfield was good, although most of the young people, thirty-five and under, went to NA or CA, because it seemed like most of the people in AA were old and redneck cowboys. I really became great friends with the people I met in those meetings and especially close with two friends, Todd and Bill. Todd was married with two young children, a boy and girl, and he was originally from Oklahoma. Bill was originally from Texas, and we spent a lot of time together outside of meetings. I sometimes think we stayed sober because we took everybody else in the meeting inventory to the point we had made up names for some of the people we thought had more problems than drinking.

To give you an example of how crazy Todd was and always making fun of the way Bill talked with his Texas accent, he had his son shake Bill's hand coming out of the mail slot in his front door. Well, Bill found out it wasn't Blake's hand; it was Todd's ding-a-ling, and oh my god, he shook it before he realized what he was shaking. We laughed over that for months, but for some reason, Bill didn't think it was that funny. During this time, my mom had moved back down south, and my dad had a young Asian girlfriend. My dad had bought her a corvette, but luckily it was in his name.

One time they were playing tennis, and I guess he thought he was thirty and not in his sixties and dove for a ball, landing on his hip and fracturing it. I don't believe they did a hip replacement, but he was in the hospital to help heal the fracture. My mom and sister were worried about him, so they came up and stayed with me in his condo. He had given me his checkbook so I could pay any bills that came in.

One Saturday evening I was visiting him, after my sister had seen him, and they found his checkbook and began to look at the book to see what he was spending money on. They already knew about the car, and I think that they suspected more money was going to his girlfriend who was half his age. Why else would she be interested in him if it was not for money? They did find out that he was buying all kinds of clothes and furniture for her house. By the time they looked at all the money he was spending on her, my mom was more than mad. She had been with him for over forty years, and he got upset with her if she bought one dress or even worse if she bought new bras. My mom got back down south and immediately got an attorney and filed for divorce. They had been separated for many years; I guess my mom was thinking, *Why spend the money on lawyers?* But after she saw what he was spending on this woman, that was the straw that broke the camel's back. Somehow my dad found out that they had found his checkbook, and when I went to visit him after they had left, he was so angry that I thought he was going to attempt to get out of bed and hit me. What he said to me I will never forget, and I think I might have had three months of sobriety, so my emotions were easily upset. He rose up and said, "You are no goddamn son of mine, and I never want to see your face again."

I left traumatized and went directly to a meeting. I shared what happened, and after the meeting, a friend came up to me and talked with me. He was an ex-con and had been sent to prison for killing someone. What he said I will never forget either. He said, "Pat, if that woman was not in his life, this would have never happened. It really is her fault. Would you like me to do her in for what she has caused?"

I said, "What do you mean do her in?"

He said, "I will have no problem shooting her to death, even if it means they find out who did it and I go back to prison."

I said, "Bill, no way! I would never be able to live with myself," and that was the end of the conversation.

I really liked the people that I grew up with in AA in Bakersfield. We became so close that I spent all my time with my sober and clean friends. There was one woman I became good friends with because I could talk to her about my girlfriend leaving me and me expecting her to come back to me when she saw that I was sober. She was married, and so there was no attraction on either of our parts, just good friends. Well, I guess her husband, who was a gang member, thought there was more going on. One evening I was in the middle of a meeting, and a person came into the room and started yelling, "Pat, get the hell out of here right now!"

Everyone stood up and said, "What is going on?"

The guy yelled, "Johnny [this woman's husband] has a gun and is looking for Pat!"

I scrambled as fast as I could to get out of there. I guess the people really calmed him down to the point that he no longer thought I was having an affair with his wife. In fact, that night I got a call at about one in the morning, and it was him calling me. He said, "Pat, I am really sorry. I found out that you are just friends with my wife, and you really want your girlfriend back. I promise you are safe with regards to me." I thanked him, and he hung up. I got on my knees and thanked God that he performed this action so fast. One more thing for me to realize how powerful God was in my life.

I had been sober for around a year and a half, and my brother came up to Bakersfield to visit my dad and had to go to court for his sentencing for drunk driving. Now my brother was more of a functioning alcoholic than me. For one thing, he graduated from college and had good jobs. But he didn't do so good when he drove. I believe this was his fifth DUI, not including the ones he got downed to reckless driving. Well, my uncle Barney was visiting my dad, making amends. He was sober, and he talked to my brother. I guess they had such a good talk he convinced my brother he was an alcoholic and took him to his first meeting in Bakersfield. When I heard what meeting he went to, I said to myself, *Oh my god, he will not relate to those old redneck drunks.* But to my surprise, he loved the meeting; and as soon as he got back down south, he went to a meeting where he met his sponsor, who was still his sponsor as of May 2020.

Since I got sober, I never had gone to a meeting down in Newport or that area, so I had no idea what the meetings were like, except what my brother would tell me over the phone. Well, the summer he had one year, he told me about this big roundup that they had in Palm Springs with thousands of drunks and I should go. So my friend Bill and I drove my dad's Corvette to the desert where we met my brother. Not only did we meet him, but we met his sponsor, Jim W., and all of their friends. I believe Jim had around fifteen years at the time, and I could not believe how awesome he was. By the time I left that convention, I was convinced I wanted what those men and women had and was ready to do anything I could to move back down to Newport. Well, I had been working as a computer analysist for the windmill farms, and Jim found out that I was very knowledgeable with computers. IBM personal computers were only out for maybe a year, and he had an appraiser friend who had computerized his office, and it made a huge difference. So Jim told my brother to come down and meet him, and maybe he would hire me to computerize his office. So I went down to my brother's, and the first thing he did was buy me some clothes that were a little more fashionable than the ones I had. So on the way to meet Jim for lunch, Mike kept telling me to be a gentleman and to please not gobble my food down in one bite, but to take my time eating as to make a good impression on Jim. We got our lunches, and before I realized it, Jim ate as fast as or faster than me, so that gave me the signal to eat like I always did. When we finished eating, it seemed like Jim and I were a match, so he hired me to computerize his office. I believe within a week, I moved back down to Newport and lived with my brother.

The first Monday I went to Jim's office, he had around five appraisers working for him, and his son John was the office manager. John and I hit it off right away, and he was not a drunk, but everyone else except for one appraiser Jim had hired from meeting them or sponsoring them through AA. Within the first week, I was stunned because everyone was so positive and upbeat and loved life.

Back then, Jim would even say, "Pat, I haven't had my best day yet. And I haven't had a bad day since I've been sober. You know how that has happened?" He told me, "Every day is twenty-four hours, and you can start the day anytime within those hours. So I may have a few bad moments, but then I start my day over, and it turns out to be a good day." Jim had asked me when I met him for lunch the first time if I had a sponsor, and I told him no. Then he said, "Pat, you need a sponsor, so I suggest getting one as soon as possible."

Probably a week later, I got Tony S. who worked for and was sponsored by Jim. The first meeting I ever attended was a speaker meeting on a Monday night in Newport, and I will never forget that meeting. These people were incredible and enjoying being sober. They were laughing belly laughs, and many times when the speaker would share, he would have to stop for a minute because they were laughing so loud and long. My god, I found out that you don't have to be a glum lot to be sober. I had not been to an actual AA meeting this fun the whole time I was in Bakersfield, and I felt this was a gift from God. I will never forget. I believe it was my third year of sobriety that many of my family came to see me receive. Even my sister and brother-in-law came. Of course my sister knew I was a raging alcoholic because I lived next to them while I was drinking heavily, and when I was in the navy, I would call her in the middle of the night all lit up. And then when I got transferred to San Diego, I would take the train to San Juan Capistrano, and she would have to put me into her car, even though it was probably less than an hour train ride to her house from San Diego. But needless to say, I never left the bar car on the train.

After only six months of living in Newport, I met so many friends that I still have thirty-four years later. Jim became not only my hero, but closer to me than I was with my own dad. He never sponsored me, but in a way I think we were closer because he was not my sponsor. When we would go to the bank together to make deposits, I would always tell the teller that he was my son, and he would say, "Thanks for the money, Dad."

I think into about my fourth year of sobriety, I was constantly getting sinus infections. So I went to an ENT doctor who was recommended to me. He said I needed rhinoplasty because of the broken noses I had had. But he wasn't sure about my sinus even though they were impacted when they did a CAT scan and MRI. I got scheduled for outpatient surgery and had the surgery done. The rhino went well, but he couldn't get all the infection out of my upper sinus cavities. I went home that evening, and the next evening I had such a high fever my brother took me to the ER. They would do a minor surgery and put a type of drain tube in my upper sinus, and I would stay in the hospital for around a week so they could give me strong antibiotics through an IV.

When I got out of the hospital, I made an appointment with the doctor at UCI. He was a young doctor and had not yet opened a private practice but was the chief of staff for the ENT department at UCI. Several months later, he would perform the first of four surgeries to get all the infection out of my upper and lower sinus cavities, which in the end would make me pain free, no more sinus headaches, and allow me to breathe.

Around the year of 1987 or 1988, the eye doctors had come out with an operation that would make it possible for me to be able to see 20/20 without glasses or contacts for the first time in my life. It was called RK surgery, and only a handful of eye surgeons performed it in its early stages. I got to have it done while it was still a new procedure because my sister at the time worked for an eye doctor. When my eyes fully recovered, it was so amazing to wake up in the middle of the night and be able to see clearly.

I think when I had about five years of sobriety, I had been working for a local computer distributer as an outside salesperson, and the major companies that I sold to were located in Houston, Austin, and Dallas, Texas. The first time I flew into Dallas, I could not believe how friendly the people were. I was supposed to fly from Dallas to Houston, but my boss said if I wanted to drive, that was fine. I wanted to drive because I not only really liked the people but also liked the wide-open country. I really got along good with my clients; and when I got back to California, my boss, the actual owner, was really happy with my sales. I worked there for maybe a little over a year.

One of the funniest episodes was when we had a lady sales representative come in to promote her product. Well, me being me, it didn't matter if it was a professional sales training course; I still had to make people laugh. So this lady was dressed in a suit, and I was jabbing the arm of one of our inside sales reps under the desk to make her laugh. She also was trying to stay sober. Well, I guess I got a little too crazy and spilled a large pitcher of coffee all over this lady's suit. I had to do everything I could not to crack up, while the owner of the company didn't think it was a bit funny and let me know that after she left, and he called me in his office. From then on, I didn't horse around when sales reps came in to promote their product.

After being there for a little over a year, I told my sponsor I was moving back to Bakersfield. He along with everyone else said, "What the hell would you want to move back up there for?" And I said I got a great job offer as a manager of a computer retail store. They all said I was crazy; but they, including my sponsor, let me move. Well, they knew exactly why I moved up there, and I was not aware of it. I moved back there because I was convinced that being sober for over five years, my girlfriend would now want to marry me. That didn't go so well, and I found myself in a bar with a few friends. Thank God they said, "Rat, we are not allowing you to take one drink, because if you attempt to, we will kick your ass." And these were friends that I used to drink with all the time. I guess it proved that they really were friends. So I went outside and got in a phone booth and called my sponsor at around one in the morning, and he answered. He had told me before never to call him after 9:00 p.m. unless I was ready to pick up a drink. When he answered, I said, "Ray, I was in a bar and almost drank. I have to tell you I didn't move up here because of the job offer. I moved up here because I thought my old girlfriend would want to marry me."

With that, he said, "Pat, no shit, we all knew why you moved back up there, and I'm so glad that you were able to get honest with yourself without having to go back out." So after we talked awhile, he told me that Jim would hire me back, and so I was back in Newport that Monday. That was one of the biggest lessons I had to learn without taking a drink. And I still get teased up for it. "Hey, Pat, are you going to leave Newport Beach and the ocean to move back up to beautiful Bakersfield?" and then they would laugh their butts off.

I never moved back up there again but would visit friends occasionally. I started working for Jim again and was loving life once again, once I got honest with myself. There is an old saying in AA, which I think came from the Bible, "To thy own self be true"; and wasn't that the truth.

There was one friend of ours who maybe had a year less than me, and he would crack us up because he would always say he was in fear. We would say, "Why?" or "What is causing your fear?" and his reply was always the same: "I don't know why. I'm just in fear." And we would laugh to ourselves.

Around the year 1995, I finally got a guy that I sponsored that finished all the twelve steps with me. When I met him, he was in a recovery program, where they lived in homes on the beach or apartment units on the beach, but the guy who owned the recovery center would put maybe four people in one room to be able to make money after he had paid the monthly rent or lease. Well, Ross had been in there for over a month, and I told him it was time to leave and live in the real world. The recovery center didn't want him to leave (money), so they told his parents he needed at least another month before he would be stable enough to live on his own. His parents called me, and I told them what I thought, and they went with my idea and saved a lot of money. I'm here to say that he got married and is very successful in his career, with one son who is fifteen and another who I believe is in his second year and playing baseball for his college. I just talked to Ross, and he just celebrated twenty-five years of sobriety. I said, "God, that is a miracle considering the first three or four years I sponsored you," and we both cracked up.

In 1995, I met Uncle Pauli and his roommates who were mostly dancers who danced around poles. One time I asked him where Verna was, and he said upstairs, and she was yelling, "Come on up, Pat!" She was in the bathtub naked talking to me, and she was very good looking.

She turned out to be like a sister to me, and a few times I would go with her on a weekend so she could make a lot of tips in Vegas.

She finally OD'd on heroin, which she had never done, and her German shepherd would not let anyone in, so Uncle Pauli and I came to the house, and I went in and got her dog, Dutch, because I was like a second owner. I couldn't keep him because we lived in a condo on the beach, and there was no room for him, but for a week, he slept on my bed and would put his big head on my chest and cry himself to sleep.

We lived in a condo where a girl from the program lived with her husband, and she had been a professional dancer before she met him, and then she didn't need to work because he made great money. She always shared what an asshole he was, but I got to know him and would realize that she was bipolar and did not take her meds, and he was a great guy and very loving to his three kids, two from a previous marriage and the youngest with Suzy. We became good friends. He owned a commercial building in Irvine that was at least 20,000 sq. ft., and I rented a space for my office, and god, we had a great time. He was built like a bodybuilder and is probably ten to fifteen years younger than me. But he got me on the Atkins diet, and for the first time since I had been in my twenties, I shredded all my love handles and had close to zero fat.

They would divorce, and he got a girlfriend that I fell in love with and was so happy for him because she was normal and also a stone fox. We became so close, and with me the blabbermouth, they would find themselves in bed, with me lying at the end of the bed, talking and talking, and they would finally say, "Pat, it's time to leave." That to me meant that they wanted to have some extra-curricular activity. I got so close with them and the kids that they started calling me Uncle. Marc owned a 16,000 sq. ft. home he was remodeling, in an exclusive area known as Orange Park Acres, and it was the most expensive and largest home I had and still the largest I have ever appraised.

I knew about Orange Park Acres because my sponsor had a 6,000 sq. ft. home on a few acres that had a view all the way to the Palisades Point on a clear day. He had two or three horses and a sheep. And I would spend three months in the winter watching his house while he was in Montana hunting, and then he would be gone most of the summer in Montana riding horses and fly fishing.

A few times I would bring up a lady, and even though they knew it wasn't my house, I would try to let them move in, which I wanted to but did not want to lose the trust Ray had for me. One time I got home in my suit, and it was usual to just feed the horses before I changed. Well, one evening I couldn't believe my eyes because it looked like a horse had kicked the sheep, and its foot was dangling off its leg. So I called a vet, and he said I had to bring the sheep to his office. I had a Volkswagen convertible, and I didn't think how I was going to put it in my car. I could just think, *Oh my god, I can't let this sheep die. Ray will kill me.* Well, I tried every imaginable way to catch this sheep; and by the time I gave up, I had more hay and horseshit on me than the damn corral had. I finally called a friend of his who lived close by, and he came and saw how worried I was and what a mess I was and started laughing his head off. I said, "Goddamn, what the hell is so funny about a sheep with its foot dangling off?"

He said, "Pat, that sheep is fine. It is just shedding its hoof." Oh my god, was I the laughingstock of AA meetings for a while.

Ray was a big game hunter and would go to Africa to get trophies. He also taught me how to use a pistol and would tell me, "If anyone breaks into this house, you better be ready to shoot because they are either totally insane or on heavy drugs." The reason he said this is that as soon as you opened the front door, there greeting you was a ten-inch stuffed brown bear; and if you went ten feet further, you would see a fully stuffed lion from Africa. He also told me that he was the hero of an African town when he shot the lion, because it would come into the town and actually drag people away and eat them. I guess like many animals, once they taste human blood, they like it.

A funny story is when I was watching his house one time, I was with Jim doing an appraisal, and we stopped at the house. Ray had a target with arrows nearby. Jim got out of the car and made a sign that said something like "Leave us animals alone," and stuck it to the target with an arrow.

Ray was very good to me besides being my sponsor. In 1987, he cosigned on a lease for me to get a little Ford Escort, which was perfect for me. I had maybe had it for a year when I was in a serious accident, and it was totaled. I was picking up a friend and had to go past the Orange County airport and was going around 50 mph. A lady in her big Jaguar was late picking up her husband and ran a red light and broadsided the driver's side. I don't remember anything except waking up in the hospital. I had received many bruises and bumps but had sustained a serious head injury that affected my life for over a year. The neurosurgeons and neurologist said it was worse because of all my previous head injuries. I was in the hospital for around seven days until the swelling went down in my brain. I would continue for follow-ups for over a year because I couldn't remember and comprehend anything I read, and I stuttered. To this day, if I get very upset, I still will sometimes stammer with my speech. I was really depressed thinking I would never be the same. But because my medical doctors and mental health doctors were so great, they kept telling me, "Patrick, all of these problems will eventually go away," and with their help, they did go away.

Some people may think I didn't have much to lose before the accident. What really amazes the doctors to this day is the fact that I have really no permanent scarring on my brain. I thank God that I don't, because they tell me most people who have the number of serious injuries that I've had to my brain are in a convalescent home, not being able to take care of themselves.

I have had such a good life being sober, and so much of it is because of the great sponsors I have had and most importantly the closeness that I have always had with Jim. He has also always hired me back, when I thought I wanted to try something besides appraising. It's funny because I love appraising and look forward to it every day I go to work, or when I started working for myself. Once I moved back down south from Bakersfield, I moved in and out of different apartments with different roommates. The best roommate I ever had was a guy who played football with my brother in junior college and at San Diego State. Sam was renting a three-bedroom, two-bath duplex, with the owners living on the second floor, and we lived on the first floor. This home was right on the sand in Newport on Seashore Drive and Forty-Eighth Street at the time. I will never forget Sam telling me and another roommate that we would never forget living on the sand. And to this day, I still remember, mainly because Samuel was such a great guy and was into martial arts, both Korean hard style and Chinese tai chi. He was a black belt and trained me one on one the entire year I lived with him. What an incredible experience. Samuel would sometimes do free demonstrations of tai chi at the Newport Beach Pier, showing people the great benefits of tai chi physically, mentally, and spiritually.

It's funny after all these years, I believe he has probably been to China and other parts of the world to focus and train with some of the greatest masters in the world, both in tai chi and in qigong. The reason it is funny is in the last three or so months, I've had the privilege to train with him via Facebook, and what a difference it has already made in my life. Years ago, back in 1995, Samuel told me, "Pat, if you could focus the energy you have that you use in a negative way with all your injuries, accidents, and health problems, in a positive way, you would be one of the healthiest persons I know." And to this day, it is amazing how it is already affecting me not only physically, but emotionally and spiritually as well.

It is funny that when I think of all my illness, it always seemed to happen when there was something that was really bothering me in the inside. The summer of 1995, I was walking on Seashore Drive in the afternoon when I got the worst headache I had ever had, and it put me down on my knees. My brother Mike saw me and took me to the ER. My blood pressure was so high I had a ministroke, and they gave me enough pain medicine to kill an elephant. After all the tests, they determined I had a "cluster" headache. They said these headaches are very rare, and generally the majority of sufferers are men. I followed up with the VA, and they have treated me ever since.

I also became friends with some of the other girls, in particular one who was Verna's best friend. One time I was visiting, and Christy called me to her room. I opened up the door, and she was naked. I knew just like Verna, she had a boyfriend; but after she told me to close the door, I knew she wanted me—*not*. Her daughter who was about eight or ten was also in the room. But we also got to be friends, and one time I took her and her daughter to Disneyland for the day, and we all had a great time.

After I moved out of Samuel's place, Uncle Pauli and I would become roommates for three or four years, living in two different places on the beach. Uncle Pauli almost dressed like he was homeless but was actually a multimillionaire owning two homes in the hills of Hollywood with views all the way to the ocean. He had been very involved with cocaine, and that is why he knew so many dancers, because he was really trying to get them to get clean and sober. Pauli was a great guy and a great roommate. The first place we lived was a duplex on the lower floor on the sand at around Fifty-Eighth Street in Newport Beach. We lived there for around six months and then moved down on the peninsula in a townhome that had another townhome; both were built together. It also had a four-car garage and was on the boardwalk, across, and faced the grass on Balboa Park, near the Balboa Pier. This was an awesome newer three-bedroom, two-and-a-half-bath townhome that was probably around 3,000 sq. ft. We lived there for at least a year or two, and while we lived there, I had received a cash settlement for a car accident, and Pauli wanted me to go in with him on a down payment and buy it. Well, the financial genius that I was, I decided to buy a Porsche instead. Pauli was not upset with me because he knew I had always wanted a Porsche. While living there, Verna would always come by and sometimes stay with us for a few days.

Around the year 1997, Pauli and I received some very bad news. We got a call that Verna had died of an overdose of heroin (she had never done before), and they knew we were good friends and asked us if we could come over to the place where she had died to try to get her German shepherd to let the police go in without having to tranquilize the dog. We got there. The dog knew us, and he came running out when I called him, and we brought him home. I really wanted to keep him, but the place we lived was not suited for him. Uncle Pauli had a small dog named Dutch, and they both always had gotten along. I had him for a week, and he would sleep with me in my bed. He would put his big head (he probably weighed at least 120 lbs.) on my chest and cry himself to sleep. My god, no wonder they say dogs are man's and in this case woman's best friend. We were glad when the breeder who sold him to Verna said he would take him back and find a good owner and not charge him for the dog. They were having Verna's memorial service at the forest lawn in Los Angeles, and for sure I was going to it and driving up with Uncle Pauli in his pride and joy, his convertible 280SL Mercedes.

I was scheduled to have outpatient sinus surgery at the VA hospital in Long Beach the day before her service, but it was not going to prevent me from attending her service. I went in the morning before she was going to be laid to rest and had the surgery. Unfortunately, they found out it was much more involved than they had anticipated, and I would not go to her service because I was admitted to the hospital and would be there two or three days. It really bummed me out, and I felt so bad that I didn't attend; but Pauli, being Pauli, an awesome person, came and visited me right on his way home from the service and told me all about it and continued to say, "Pat, you didn't have a choice. Don't worry, Verna knew your heart was there."

When Pauli and I moved out, we moved into a single-family home that was owned by a woman who also was in AA. I believe I lived there maybe a year or a little less and at the time started having seizures. The doctors felt they were caused by all my previous head injuries. Around 1997, I started waking up having severe pain in my groin. I would go to the ER several times before I got an appointment with the urology department at the VA. They started trying to figure out what was causing the groin pain and finally thought it was coming from one of my testicles. So they scheduled me for surgery and removed my left testicle. Well, not even a month later, I started having the groin pain again. They did so many tests and still couldn't figure out what was causing them. The chief of staff at the VA for urology also had a private practice, and he referred me to his associate who was just starting to do experimental implants for pain that normally were used for patients who had lost the ability to control their bladder. He would put an electric implant in my butt, and it was a device that I could control the amount of electrical stimulation on my sacral nerve. It seemed to work great, and then about six months or a year later, it didn't seem to be working as well. So he decided to put a second implant on the other side of my butt. Just to be clear, they were implanted below the butt muscle. The second did the trick, and I could stop the pain completely by turning this implant on. Every few years he would have to go back in and do surgery to replace the batteries.

I will never forget one time my mom and I were visiting Bob and Marcia in Colorado Springs. I had to tell security not to run their wand around me because it could not only damage the device, but damage me as well. Well, Bob, with his great ideas and liking to joke around, had my controller when I was being searched by security. He tried to control the frequency and got it as high as it would go, because he wanted to see me dance. Thank God he didn't realize that the controller had to be against my butt hitting the internal implant to control the frequency. We all were laughing so hard I thought I would have to turn it up high so I didn't piss may pants, even though that was not the purpose of having them.

In 2000, I moved into a little studio apartment in Costa Mesa that my brother's fiancée had been living in. At the time, it was all I needed and very convenient and close to shopping and local restaurants. Marc and Rita had moved into their estate in Orange Park Acres, and I would visit them quite a bit. Living in a little studio and then going to visit them in a 16,000 sq. ft. home was, to say the least, a little overwhelming. In 2001, Marc had asked Rita to marry him, and they were getting married on a cruise ship. He asked me to be his best man, so I went on my first cruise. We flew from LAX to Florida and then spent one night before we boarded the ship. It was a seven-day cruise to the Caribbean and was a great experience, especially since I had never been on one before. The day of the wedding was taking place before we set sail, and there is one story I will never forget. Marc and I and his sons and another gentleman who was also a best man were all getting ready for the wedding. All of a sudden, just before we were to go to the location of the wedding, Marc started looking for his jacket and could not find it.

After a while, it got serious because none of us could find it. Then he was looking at me with a weird expression. He said, "Pat, that jacket is too big for you. That is my jacket."

I looked at him and said, "No, Marc, this fits me perfect."

Again, he said, "No, take that jacket off. It is mine." He finally convinced me it was his and mine was lying on a chair when I looked down and the sleeves were at least six inches longer than my hands. I wasn't sure if he was going to hit me or laugh so hard he was going to piss his pants. Thank God it was an awesome wedding, and there were no other hiccups. It went off perfect, and Rita looked stunning, to say the least.

8

Marriage

When we got back, I sold my Porsche and bought a little four-door Volkswagen sedan. There was a great little Italian restaurant that I started going to because I could walk to it, and I also noticed there was a very cute waitress who worked there and always brought me my food. I kept trying to see if she had a ring on her finger, and one night I didn't see one. Well, I'm very shy when it comes to asking someone out, except when I drank; and then I didn't care if they said yes or no. I guess I drank so much tea that the cooks were telling Ivy, "This guy wants to ask you out," and she would say no. They were all Hispanic, and I did not have a clue what they were saying. But finally she said, "Could you please pay your bill because we are closing." By that time, it was perfect timing because I was the only customer left. I said, "Are you married?" and she said no. Then I said, "Do you have a boyfriend?" and she said no. So I wrote my phone number with my name on a piece of paper and said, "If you would like to go out for lunch or dinner sometime, please give me a call." With that, I left and went home.

This was a Friday night, and to my surprise, she called me Saturday night at around nine o'clock (thank God I didn't party anymore), and she said, "Would you like to take me to lunch tomorrow?" and you know what I said. So she told me to meet her on two cross streets. I got there early and parked in a small church parking lot near the place she told me to pick her up. After about ten minutes after the allotted time, I saw this young woman walking by; but I said, *Oh my god, that can't be her. She is too young and beautiful.* I had never seen her in clothes, I mean regular clothes, and she had her long hair down.

I realized it was her, and she got in my car, and we drove to Seal Beach near the Seal Beach Pier and ate at a nice restaurant that looked out at the pier, the beach, and the ocean. I didn't know that she didn't speak or understand English very well, so me being me, it's lucky she didn't understand. Because after we had eaten and I was on about my fourth glass of iced tea, out came from my mouth (I still can't believe I said this) "Did you know that iced tea makes me very horny?"

And with that she said, "Did you know orange juice makes me—" and just then, the waitress walked up with our bill, and I finished for her, "Yes, orange can make you thirsty." She did not understand what I said or what horny meant. So we walked on the pier, and she was hesitant about letting me hold her hand, but she did, and we walked by a homeless guy sitting on a bench. We walked by and stood looking at the ocean when for some reason, she asked me if I had any change. I said, "Sure." I had no idea why she wanted it, but I gave her a $5 bill. The next thing I knew, she was talking to the homeless guy and handing him the five. At that moment, I will never forget I said, *I'm marrying this woman.*

Now I should mention I was forty-eight at the time and six months earlier had a talk with God and said, "Okay, I'm comfortable being single if that is what you want me to be," and I stopped trolling for a potential wife. Well, four months later, we were in Las Vegas by ourselves getting married in a little chapel off the strip. I knew I was taking on a family because at the time, she had a daughter who was five and an elder daughter who was sixteen. I told her that I would treat those girls as if they were my own or I would have never asked her to marry me. When we got married, she was working three different jobs and was illegal. I told her she no longer had to work. She could raise her daughters, and I would work.

We had not been married for even six months when I started getting seizures again. The first one I guess I had was on our stairs, and luckily there was a little pad between the upper and the lower portions of the stairs. I guess my wife was yelling at Deli to call an ambulance and was trying to wake me up. Well, Little Ivy was there with her, and I recognized her voice. The ambulance put me in the back with my wife, and they put Little Ivy up front. I guess Little Ivy was really upset, so they took a few gloves and made balloons with them to try to distract her. Due to these seizures becoming more and more frequent and me seeing different doctors, I would be admitted to UCLA and stay as an inpatient for a month for them to try to determine what was causing them and what part of my brain was being affected by them.

After a month, they had me stabilized with a few different anti-seizure medications. They finally determined that these grand mal seizures were caused by all the head traumas I had sustained during my life. It was a very long and trying month, because my wife went back to work, helping a sister who had her own business, and she never could visit me, mainly because she didn't know how to drive and so couldn't get up there to see me. So for the whole month I didn't see my family, and it was driving me crazy. When I finally got home, it looked like I had been in a war from all the IVs they had to put in me and all the friggin' different tests they did on me. I was totally worn out when I got home and probably didn't go back to work for two weeks after I got home.

We got married in April of 2002; and for two years, I was extremely busy, doing twenty-five to thirty appraisals in a month and driving all the way to San Diego, San Bernardino, Riverside, and the valley in Los Angeles. Fortunately, since I worked for myself, every few months Ivy and I would take an excursion to Las Vegas for two or three nights and see a show or two. I'm not a big gambler, so we would just eat and see shows and enjoy the pool. One time we brought Little Ivy and her friend with us to Las Vegas. This is again a story I will never forget. We were eating at a buffet, and my wife had gone to get some food, while Little Ivy and her friend remained at the table eating. Anyone who knows me knows that I don't chew; I swallow my food. I was eating, and all of a sudden, some food got stuck in my throat. For the first time in my life, I could not get it dislodged; and I literally started choking to death to the point that when my wife heard the commotion, I was turning blue. Thank God the people next to us saw what was happening, and a big guy grabbed me off my chair and did the Heimlich maneuver on me, and out popped a large piece of steak. This choking was so bad that I could barely swallow for a month afterward and didn't eat fast for at least until six months later, when I started eating like I always did, fast.

Candy was more the mom for Little Ivy than her mom, and she was being more of the mom than her own mom. Right from the start, I hired an attorney to get her legal as a permanent resident and then go for citizenship. After close to $15,000 in attorney's fees and one month in Ciudad Juarez (at the time, the cartels were taking over the city), she got her papers. But what an experience, because we thought we could start the process, and then we would go to Ensenada, and she could stay there, and I could cross the border and be back working and watching the girls. Well, that idea stopped the same day we drove into the city. We were lucky because several people told my wife, "You're not going to try to drive to Ensenada. First, because it's too far away, and second and most important, you will never make it without the cartels killing you and taking whatever you have including the car." So we found an inexpensive hotel that was being remodeled, and we got a great rate for the month we were there.

Once we got there, there was no guarantee that they would approve her for a permanent residence status. So it was nerve-wracking not knowing, and about the second day there, we passed a car that had been all shot up surrounded by the federals, and there was a dead guy or two riddled with bullets on the ground. That was the last time we took an excursion in the car. The consulate and everything else we needed were within walking distance, and my car was actually safe because there was a gated underground garage where it stayed parked. Well, at least I saved on gas.

We initially lived in an apartment that they shared with a cousin, but when we got married, the cousin moved out. It was a nice two-bedroom, two-bath second-level apartment. When we had been married about two years, in 2004 I had my normal urology test and had my blood work done. When I went in for my appointment, my doctor sat Ivy and me down and said, "I have some tough news for you. Your PSA level is always less than 1, and this blood work shows it at 10. I'm going to draw blood now and get the results before you leave so I know for sure that the first one was accurate." The second one indicated my PSA was 12. He was worried and wanted me to schedule an appointment so he could do a biopsy. So a week later, I went in, and he took a biopsy. A few days later, he asked us to come in the next day so he could go over the results with us. He then told us that my biopsy showed that I had cancer of the prostate. But he said, "I hate to say this, but we believe in all likelihood that it has spread to other glands." He wanted me to have chemotherapy before he removed the prostate.

I thought about it, and the next appointment I asked him, "Doctor, if it hasn't spread, if you remove the prostate, that is the end of the cancer," and he said yes. Well, I decided not to go through with chemo, because I knew that also killed the good cells, so I was scheduled to have surgery. Before I had surgery, maybe two or three months later, when we saw him, he said, "I actually have good news. All the labs and blood work now show that the cancer is only located in the prostate, so when we remove it, the cancer will hopefully all be gone." When we were scheduling for the surgery, he told us that he had to schedule the surgery three months out, because I had to give a pint of my blood every month so he would have three units of blood before the operation. We were told that it was a surgery where more blood was lost than any other type of surgery, and that is why they needed the three units of my blood. The night before my surgery, Little Ivy who was seven or eight decided she was going to do the surgery. So she was in all her doctor outfit and had me on the couch with covers over my stomach. She performed the surgery, and out came a baby. Ha-ha. It was one of her dolls, but I called the baby an "it," because I said it was half human and half rat! BA.

The day of the surgery, she would not let them take me into pre-op without her with me. So they let her and my wife both into pre-op. They usually only allow one person, but Little Ivy was so persistent and upset that they finally gave up and let her be with me during the pre-op.

I guess the surgery took longer and was more complicated than normal. I lost so much blood that they had to give me three more units of donated blood. When I was coming to, I was in a lot of pain, like everyone who had had a prostatectomy. They kept doing blood tests on me every few hours, and my wife finally asked, "Why do you keep taking his blood?" I was so out of it I had no idea what was going on. The hospital called my doctor, and he came in to talk to my wife at around seven that night. He told her, "Patrick is continuing to lose more blood, and we have no idea why. I have to tell you something that could be bad news for you. If he continues to lose the blood at the rate he is, we will have to go back in and find out where the bleeding is coming from so we can stop it. The tough part is that he is already losing too much blood, and if we operate again, he is likely to lose more blood, and he can ill afford to lose any more." What he was actually telling her was that my chances of living were not too good if they had to go back in on me. I guess my wife left, and they had a prayer meeting at her church, and she said at least fifty people showed up. My doctor called my wife that night at about eleven and said, "Ivy, I have great news. We don't know why, but the bleeding has stopped." Needless to say, my wife knew, because she felt it was a miracle from God; and after being told, I also believe it was a miracle.

This surgery really impacted my life for good. They told me that if the wrong nerves were cut, I could possibly lose the control of my bladder and have to have a catheter for the rest of my life. Then even worse, I guess they said it could also cause me to not be able to get an erection (or what I call a boner). Ha-ha. Well, I was feeling sorry for myself in November because I still was wearing diapers. I got on my computer, and for some reason (God), I found Brett Favre's website. I started reading a story about a little boy, Christopher, who lived in Texas and was dying from inoperable brain tumor. He has used up his gift of life, and so he couldn't see Brett play before he died. He and his mom were avid fans of Green Bay.

Well, guys got together and got him a ticket to a playoff game, and I with some other people paid for his hotel and flight expenses, so he got to see Brett play. Unbeknownst to him or his mother, on Saturday, they invited them to watch them practice. Wait, it gets better! Not only did he go into the training room to eat lunch with him. I found out that Brett spent more than an hour talking to this little guy. (Now you know why I'm not only a huge Packer fan, but even a bigger fan of Brett's.) What an awesome man. More athletes need to take after Mr. Favre. Then on Sunday, the day of the game, they even had a bigger surprise. They were given field passes and stood on the sidelines with the team. Now the moment to shed a tear. When Brett was warming up and throwing passes to his receivers, all of a sudden, out of nowhere, they saw this little five- or six-year-old running as fast as he could and jumping into Brett's arms. To tell you the truth, it got to me so much that I can't even remember if the Packers won the game.

Later when the boy passed away, another fan and I went to Odesa, Texas, to represent the fans of Green Bay. Even before this, Brett had texted me thanking me for helping get this little guy to Green Bay to watch him play. Then I got a text from both Brett and his sweet wife thanking me for representing the Packers and attending his memorial. God, I had only been a Packer fan for a few months, and now I found myself being the biggest fan of the Packers and even a bigger fan of Brett's. My god, what an awesome man he is. He and his wife could not attend; but the flowers they had delivered, my god, I have never seen so many flowers. Those few months are going to live with me for the rest of my life, and you can believe I'm the biggest Packer fan to this day.

With regard to my prostate surgery, I had pretty much fully recovered by December, and all my functions were working properly, at least that is what my wife told me…ha-ha. Christmas Day came, and they told me to open my gifts first. The first present I unwrapped was a Thomas Guide. I thought to myself, *Why the hell a Thomas Guide?* Well, the next present was a tape measure, and the next was a fifty-foot tape measure. Then I started laughing my ass off and said to Ivy, "Are you telling me it's time to get off the pity pot and go back to work?"

Oh, I forgot to mention that my biggest client at the time I had billed for over $5,000, and he said he would pay me before the surgery so I wouldn't have to worry about finances while I recovered. I was starting to get angry because my wife was selling so much ice cream and junk food, it didn't seem like I was getting any rest. Finally one morning, being the mellow person I am, especially if I'm in pain, I came out from my room and yelled, "What the hell is going on! Have we turned into a 7-Eleven?"

With that, my wife teared up and said we had never received a check from my client. It was only a week or so since I had been home, so I was weak and in a lot of pain. The next thing she saw was me dressed, sort of, and walking out the door. I thought she was going to faint and said, "You can't even make it down the stairs. Where are you going?"

I said, "I'm going to their office to get my money that was promised to us." She didn't drive at the time but drove with me. To this day, I'm not sure how we even made it there let alone got home. I went into their office a little upset. Well, upset enough that the owner came out of his office. He said, "Patrick, what are you doing here? You look like hell."

I said, "I never got paid like I was promised."

He looked at the woman behind the counter and said, "You never cut him a check like I promised?" I'm not sure what she said to him, but five minutes later, I received a check, and I think as I remember he added $500 and told me he was very, very sorry. He even offered to drive me home, because I looked so bad, but I said I was fine, and we made it home, although I needed my wife and a few friends to make it up the stairs and back to my bed.

We lived in the same apartment for the first three to five years of our marriage; and then I contacted a friend, Brian, who owned some apartments and rented a nice two-level, three-bedroom, two-bath apartment with a two-car built-in garage. It was perfect for the four of us; the girls had their own rooms. We had not lived there for even a month when Brian asked if Ivy would want to manage the apartment complex we lived in and also many duplexes and triplexes along with other multilevel apartments. So in exchange for rent, he trained her to manage all his properties. Unfortunately, and I'm not placing any blame on Brian, she was convinced that if he had *one* vacancy, he would lose everything. I told her after six months that she was not a doctor and was not being paid as a doctor, so she should stop working 24/7. I didn't realize how stressed she was when a few years later, I found her hiding in the bushes in front of our house, thinking about how she was going to end her life. I had her admitted into the hospital that night, and she would be placed in an in-house hospital treatment center for a month. They also at the time diagnosed her with extreme depression. I continue to thank God that I found her before she did something to herself.

A good story, however, was that when we lived there, Candy would meet the man that she would marry. It's funny because after the first date, I said, "Wow, you guys got home early," and they were in his car in front of the house for a long time. I asked her how her date was, and she said, "We had a great time at dinner, and then we got home, and he spent the next few hours reading the Bible and explaining it to me."

My wife was a Christian, and around the year 2005, Little Ivy and I were baptized in the ocean at Big Corona in Corona del Mar. Well, the next date, I asked how it went, and the same response: "We had a nice dinner and then spent a few hours in front of the house reading the Bible." He would always be so polite when bringing her to the front door.

I would tell my wife, "Well, thank God Francisco is a good Christian. At least he is not a drunk like me or likes to do a little social heroin." This dating went on for probably two months, and one day when he came in after their date, I said, "Francisco, I'm sorry, but I'm giving you a new name." Everyone looked at me and probably was thinking, *Oh my god, what has Patrick come up with now?* Well, I told him his new name was BB, short for Bible Boy; and to this day, that is what I call him. They would have a son named Jayden, and within two or three months, we knew something wasn't right. He would be diagnosed with autism; and thank God the regional center, the same as where my dad opened the second hospital in Bakersfield, started having a therapist come in the house twice a week. Deli and BB and the baby would live with us until he was around three years old, and then they got their own apartment.

I have to be honest: I did not know how Deli and BB could deal with all their son's screaming and tantrums, because it was bad enough on me, even though I would go to our room and shut the door. This boy to this day is the apple of my eye and is the son I never had. In addition, what an awesome, awesome experience to have a child who has a challenging disability live with you. I am here to tell you that he has taught me way more than I could ever teach him. For example, it used to drive me crazy when I was in a public place, grocery store, eating out when a child would have a tantrum. Now with my eyes open, if someone says something to a mother with an unruly child, I pull them aside, and a miracle for me I don't get upset and yell. I just let them be aware of the fact that this child may have some type of disability, and even if they don't, I tell them please have some patience and tolerance for both the mother and child. Thank you, God, for putting Jayden into my life and continuing to teach me patience, kindness, and love. He now has a sister who is three years old, and Jayden is eight, and he takes care of her like she is his most important assignment.

My wife and I or one of us usually goes to his school at least once a month ever since he was in first grade to give him his favorite, a McDonald's meal. Well, now he is eight and weighs around 90 lbs., so it is not only a happy meal, but at least one double cheeseburger, with fries, and nothing else on the burger but cheese. In addition, he will generally spend Friday and Saturday nights with us at least once a month and usually twice if I can kidnap him from his mom and dad. I act like his mom and I are divorced, and I call her and say, "Okay, it's my weekend. Ha-ha."

In 2008, I started having chronic cluster headache attacks and was finally sent from the VA pain clinic to UCLA to be seen by some of the best neurologists, neurosurgeons, and radiology doctors that can be found. They did so many tests and diagnostics to try to get these headaches to stop. The problem was that they would cause so much pain that my blood pressure would skyrocket, and due to this fact, I have had over three ministrokes. Thank God there was no permanent damage, although some people might question that. Ha-ha. They finally did a few surgeries where they would go into an area that was located just outside the sac that protects your brain and do some type of treatment that I didn't understand but didn't care because I was knocked out.

Unfortunately, none of these worked, and they were really worried that I would eventually have a major stroke caused by them. They finally talked to radiology and decided to do nine treatments of Gamma Knife surgery. They planned on doing it nine different times. However, that would change because they found when they were trying to do a CAT scan that they couldn't complete it because I would get vertigo so severe that I would throw up. Thank God the first time since I was strapped to the bed and yelling at them that I was getting sick to my stomach, they pulled me out in time to projectile vomit all over them instead of maybe choking to death because I would choke on my own vomit if I wasn't able to get on my side. I really felt bad when I saw two of the nurses covered and I mean covered in my vomit. I couldn't believe it. When I was sitting on the table, I was crying like a baby because I felt so bad vomiting on them. One of the nurses covered in my vomit kept saying, "Please, Patrick, stop being so upset. We can take a shower here and put on new scrubs." It was so awesome how they all treated me with love and compassion.

What would happen was that they would have to have an anesthesiologist come in and put me completely out so they could do the CAT scans that would help them make a full mask that they could tighten down on the table when they did these procedures. The only good thing that came out of this was instead of having to do nine separate procedures, since I was knocked completely out, they could do three each time I had treatment; so I only had to have three treatments that would last over an hour each, instead of nine that would only take fifteen to thirty minutes. After everything, they tried including Gamma Knife. I was still having severe cluster headaches. I have to mention they tried every medicine ever given to someone to stop cluster headaches, and nothing worked.

After these procedures, my neurosurgeon made an appointment for me and my wife to see him. So the day of the appointment, he called my wife and me into his office. He had us sit down and told us no one in neurology, and even after talking with physicians from Cal Berkeley and Stanford, had come across a case as difficult as mine. He proceeded to tell us that they were out of options and that I would have to take Dilaudid the rest of my life, to get rid of the pain, so I wouldn't have a stroke. The fortunate thing that they did not understand was that even after a year, the same dose was working. They said it was very unusual because most patients, especially on this pain medication (according to them, the strongest pain medicine they can give), would be constantly running out and asking for more.

So thank God for the next four years (2008–2012) I would continually have to take this medicine for each headache, and sometimes I would have four or five a day, and they would last anywhere from two hours up to four hours for each headache. The other amazing thing is that I didn't build up a tolerance, so I would not have the high and euphoria that most patients experience. To get back to the topic, the doctor told us, "Patrick, you only have one option besides the pain medicine to control your pain. That option is now experimental surgery, where we go into the brain and put an electronic stimulator on the hypothalamus where this headache originates."

He said, "You and your wife think about your options, and I will schedule an appointment for you next week." I did my due diligence and found that over 90 percent of the people who had this surgery were having grand mal seizures, and they were sometimes so severe that some of the patients were having brain damage because of the surgery. When we went back to see him, we told him that we had discussed at length and had decided the best option for me was to continue with treating them with pain medication. He told us that was fine with him and that he felt I was very fortunate that I was able to take the same dose even after a year, and he was confident that I would never have to increase it. When we researched the type of surgery, we found he had invented it and was probably regarded as the top neurosurgeon in all of Brazil, where he had a large clinic for people with chronic pain from headaches, and was one of the few and best in the world for treating cluster headaches. After 2012, the headaches stopped and would only occur a few times a year for maybe a week, which was typical for people who suffer this type of headaches. The doctor also told us that they never have found why certain people suffer these headaches, and fortunately, there are few people who get them, and that is one of the reasons that there are not a lot of treatment options, because they are so rare, and it is hard to get grants to study them.

In 2013, I was at the gym lifting weights when I heard a pop in my groin and suddenly had pain in that area. I went to the restroom and felt down in my groin and could tell there was a lot of swelling, so due to the discomfort, I stopped working out and went home. That night I was really in discomfort, so I made an appointment to see my doctor. A few days later, the urologist at the VA told me I had a lower hernia, and I needed to make an appointment with general surgery to have it operated on. So they would do an open surgery, not laparoscopic or robotic surgery, I guess because the hernia was so large. It was outpatient surgery, and the worst part about it was that I could not work out for six to eight weeks, and I always have worked out four to six times a week ever since I have been married. I found that it really helps me with stress, depression, and anxiety, better than any pill they would give me.

I would have another upper hernia a few years later, and once again it was open surgery as an outpatient, and I would not be able to work out for six to eight weeks.

In 2016, I was rushed to the hospital with a really bad headache. They did all the tests and found I had some kind of embolism that broke. Fortunately, once again, there was no apparent brain damage; but it caused me to be blind in my right eye. They finally called in an eye surgeon to see if he could find the cause of the blindness. He examined me and said I had a detached retina that required him to do surgery. He told me matter-of-factly that since it occurred over five days previous, the likelihood of regaining any vision in that eye was remote. If they get to a detached retina within the first twenty-four to forty-eight hours, the success rate is good; but after that, every twenty-four hours makes a big difference in the success of the operation. So he told my wife and me to not be optimistic with the outcome of the surgery. He was right because when they took the band off the eye, I still had no vision, which he predicted, so I wasn't shocked with the outcome, but I was depressed that I would never have vision in that eye.

Maybe six months later, he referred me to a doctor who specialized in contract surgery, and I had a contract in that eye. So I went and saw her, and I can tell you that even with one eye, this doctor was gorgeous, and I thought, *Is that really a doctor, or is she a model of some kind?* Well, she was the doctor, and I had a crush on her, even though I was married. Ha-ha. She scheduled me for surgery, and once again, she told me not to expect any miracle after the surgery. The next day I went in for her to examine the eye, and before she took off the bandages over the eye, once again she said, "Patrick, please don't expect any or little improvement in your vision." She took off the bandages, and the first thing that came out of my mouth was "Oh my god, Doctor, you are the most beautiful doctor I have ever seen," and I swear the two of us started crying. Well, maybe she only teared up, but I cried because I had almost perfect vision in that eye. Unfortunately, as the years went by, the vision got worse; and today if I put my hand my arm's distance, I am lucky if I can make out the separation of my fingers. But I still love to see her, because she is so pretty. Unfortunately for me, she has a boyfriend; and in addition, I am old enough to be her dad, not her boyfriend. Ha-ha.

After we had moved to Huntington Beach, I was thrilled since I could ride my bike easily to the beach. One day I decided to go bodysurfing, which I probably had not done in ten years. The waves were not big, but the surf was still probably four to five feet, and I was not used to bodysurfing. So I took off on a wave, and it ground me into the sand. Thank God I still remembered to duck to avoid any potential neck injury. But I came up with a lot of discomfort in my shoulder. The next day I went to my doctor and found out I needed surgery for a torn rotator cuff, and pieces of bone needed to be removed. I had to go to physical therapy for probably eight weeks and once again could not go to the gym.

In 2014, I received back pay from the VA and had enough money to come up with a down payment for a townhome, condo, or home in Riverside or San Bernardino counties. We really considered the mountains, including Big Bear, but the more we thought about it, the more we decided we couldn't move into a cold climate because Ivy suffered from an immune disease that caused great pain in all her joints, and the cold would not be good for her. So I said to her, "Ivy, I have lived near the ocean all my life; and if we have to rent the rest of our lives, then so be it, because I refuse to live inland." We also had the option to move to Oregon or Washington State, but again, those places would not be conducive to her condition, so they also were not an option.

Being a real estate appraiser for over thirty years, for a few years I started specializing in appraising mobile homes. My mom had one, and they were built with two-by-two framing, and the inside walls were made up of thin paneling. She had her inside totally remodeled, and it actually looked like a typical stick home, even though it wasn't.

After a few years of appraising these mobile homes, I began to notice that they were more and more being built like regular homes with two-by-four framing, and the interior walls were made up of drywall. In fact, I appraised one in the desert, and it was on a typical foundation for a home, and when you saw it, even up close you would never guess that it was a manufactured home. It even had a wood-burning fireplace and was financed as a regular single-family residence.

The more I investigated, the more I became interested in purchasing one because I could still be near the water. Several months after getting the money, we found a perfect home in an awesome mobile home park that was family friendly. So we bought a home, and it went into escrow. Escrow closed, and we were living in a motel for a few days, while it was still in escrow. My wife went by the house a few days before it was due to close and called me and said the police basically had it surrounded. I rushed to the park and found out that there was a squatter who had moved into the home, and it was a difficult situation to get her out, if they could get her out. We were between a rock and a hard place because we were in a hotel with everything we owned in a U-Haul truck.

The realtor called me and asked me to come look at another home on the same street that she had listed. I went through and inspected the home and told the realtor I thought it was nice, but I didn't think my wife would like the floor plan. She then told me that she would reduce the price and give us this home for the same price we were paying for the squatter's house. I was very apprehensive, but I called Ivy and told her to come over and look at the home, especially since she knocked down the price by $15,000. So she came and looked at the house and to my amazement loved the floor plan, even much more than the squatter's home, so the realtor put it in escrow. Fortunately, the previous owner turned out to be a great guy and said we could move into the house the following day and just pay for the month's lease payment. So we moved into it the following day, and now the year 2020, we still have it. In fact, I myself painted the exterior, even though it took me most of the summer. Ivy never saw me on the high ladder, painting the top boards, or she would have had a shit attack.

In fact, this cat turned into my dog because it would follow me everywhere I went. It is now around seventeen or eighteen years old and has been an indoor cat ever since we moved into this house. I love this cat like no other pet I have ever had, and she knows it. I think animals realize when they have been rescued from an abuser and love you even more. This jackass who had this cat would kick it when it would throw up a hair ball. He is very lucky that I didn't beat the shit out of him when I found out. This kitty cat started coming into our backyard, and we would feed her. The problem was we had another cat that was maybe four or five, and when she would go into the backyard and Gordo would be there, Gordo would try to play with him, and she would yell and scream like she was being raped, and Gordo just wanted to play with him.

They eventually started to get along, although Precious (a boy, but Little Ivy named him) still would cry bloody murder if Gordo even got near him. The guy who had Gordo was moving and came to our door and told me he wanted his cat back. Thank God I've mellowed out, and I told him to get off our porch before he would find himself in the hospital. Then I calmed down and said, "Okay, you can pay me back for all the food and vet bills that we have paid— *not*! You will never get this cat back, you piece of work." I added, "If you ever come close to our apartment again, I hope the police show up before I do something that is going to land me in jail, and to tell you the truth, you're not worth going to jail over." If you can't tell, I dislike anyone who abuses any animal, domestic or wild. They show such amazing unconditional love; it's too bad we humans don't have the same capacity for love.

I believe what I have learned about dogs. You reverse the letters, and you have *God*. Jesus tried his best to teach us that living was all about unconditional love for everyone. I call myself a Christian, but I never have put any kind of sticker on my car indicating I am a Christian or for that matter a sticker indicating I don't drink, for fear that I might get angry and flip someone off while driving. I have to admit though at least for the last five or seven years, I have done what my brother Mike taught me for road rage, when someone does something stupid while driving. Instead of flipping them off, I give them the peace sign, and many times it makes them even angrier, and I have to admit I love it. I think I might get angrier than most drivers when they see someone run a red light or do something that could cause a serious accident, because I was severely injured twice in car accidents caused by someone who was not paying attention while they were driving.

One time I got very emotional when I saw a man driving in front of me with a picture of his deceased twenty-four-year-old daughter, stating, "Don't text and drive. You might kill someone like my beautiful daughter." I guess it's true when people have told me I wear my emotions on my sleeve because when we both stopped at a red light, I got out of my car very gently and carefully, and I went up to his car, crying like a baby and saying, "Oh my god, I'm so sorry for your loss," and he started to cry, saying, "It still affects me so deeply even though she lost her life over two years ago." He sincerely thanked me, and we both said a prayer for her. Other drivers nearby gave me a thumbs-up when they saw what had occurred and noticed how affected I was by his decal.

I can honestly say that with so many of my life experiences that have occurred, they are not coincidences but I believe they are direct results of divine intervention.

It's not coincidental that this last story is the biggest miracle that has occurred in my life.

In September of 2018, I had a bad cough that was diagnosed as bronchitis, and I was given a Z-Pak to get rid of it. After the Z-Pak ran out (maybe five days), a week later the cough got worse with a fever. So they did all the x-rays, CAT scan, and MRI and found out I had a small case of pneumonia (walking pneumonia); so they put me on stronger antibiotics and said if it had not cleared in a week, they would probably have to admit me to the hospital so they could give me even stronger antibiotics through IVs. Fortunately, after a week, the fever and cough were gone. They scheduled me to have another x-ray along with MRI and CAT scan in December because they had seen a small spot in one of my lungs, and they wanted to make sure it was gone. So around five months later, in December, I was scheduled once again to see my doctor and have the test done. The appointment was on December 17 in the afternoon, so as usual I worked out and then proceeded to the doctor's office. When I checked in, the nurse sort of had a puzzled look and said, "Mr. McNeese, do you feel okay?"

And I said, "Oh, I actually feel great. I just had a great workout before coming here."

One of the doctors happened to walk by to go to another section of the clinic, and she looked at me and said, "Get this man to a room immediately." The next thing I knew, I was surrounded by nurses and doctors, and they put an oxygen mask on me. Then all of a sudden, a couple of guys who drove an ambulance put me on their gurney and transported to the nearby Hoag Hospital emergency room. Then I started to have a high fever, and my wife was there. Although I had such a high fever, I didn't know what was going on. She told me later that they said I had serious pneumonia and then developed the flu. I remember the next morning being in a private room in the hospital, and that is all I remember, until three weeks later when I woke up from an induced coma. I had gotten what is called septic shock in my blood that day, and it eventually shuts down all your organs, most importantly your ability to breathe. So waking up three weeks later, I found out that not only had I been on life support, but I had flatlined (died three times because my heart stopped) in the first forty-eight hours of being on life support. They told my wife at that time that my chances of living were very remote and that she should be aware that me passing away was very probable. Thank God I made it to three weeks, and then the doctors met with my family and told them, "Patrick has been on life support for three weeks, and his chances of living would be a miracle, and so we recommend that we take him off life support tomorrow morning and let him pass away peacefully."

So they agreed with the doctors and would be there at six in the morning to witness me passing away. This is another miracle: around two in the morning, my wife was there, and I started to breathe on my own. By six in the morning, when they were to disconnect me and let me die, they did disconnect at about the same time, but I was breathing on my own and no longer needed the machines to keep me alive. So that day I woke up surrounded by my family and did not have a clue what had happened. They would tell me in little bits at a time what had happened because they didn't want to overwhelm me telling me everything that had happened at once. I remained at Hoag for another week, then they transferred me to a subacute hospital.

When I arrived at this hospital, I weighed 126 lbs. and had weighed 185 lbs. when I went to my doctor's appointment in December. I would stay in this hospital until March 1, when I was released and sent to a convalescent hospital. I would remain in this hospital with a tracheotomy, and they fed me intravenously until they felt I could eat on my own. They finally pulled the trac, and I could start eating pudding. They would do swallowing tests on me every week, and I kept failing them, so I stayed on this diet until the last week I was there. I became addicted to pudding to the point where the nurses would have to go to different nurses' stations, even on different floors, to find pudding that would suffice until the next morning. While I was there, I tried to get out of my bed, because the nurses would not come when I pressed the call button. The nurses' station was right in front of my room, and I was yelling at them, and they still did not come. Well, I got fed up; and even though I had not been on my feet for over two months, I attempted to get out of my bed. It didn't work, because I came crashing down at once and would hit an IV pole that scratched my eye and left a large scar on my right eye. I was discharged, and I had no vision in my right eye when I arrived at the convalescent hospital.

I was so grateful to be there, because the entire staff was incredible and really cared for me. The amazing part is that all the staff, including all the physical therapists, thought I would be there for at least a month before I could go home. Well, to my amazement and theirs, I went home after being there for only a week. This staff was so incredible I attribute my quick recovery to them. But they would tell me I recovered so fast because I was in great shape before I got sick, and that shows people that even when you're knocking at death's door, it really matters what kind of shape your body is in to make a full recovery. They sent physical therapists and nurses to my home every day and would work with me mainly to get my strength back. To their amazement, they only visited me for two weeks, and they thought I would need them for at least a month. Again, I astonished them; and once again, they all said it was because I was in such great shape before I got sick. They left me with a walker and said to use it for a month before trying to walk without it. I was walking with my wife and got to the point that I could walk around the entire complex without needing a rest. And within two weeks, I was walking without any walker and just having my wife to lean on if I got tired.

I will never forget the date of April 8, 2019, because it was my first day back at 24 Hour Fitness, and all the staff went crazy because they had heard about my condition, and they were stunned to see me back so soon. By August, I was back up to 180 lbs. and working out like I did before I got sick. It really is a miracle that the only lasting side effect I had from this long journey of being dead and coming back was that I lost the sight of my right eye (I cannot see my fingers at arm's distance). Another thing I found out is that somehow I was declared dead, and many of my banks, credit unions, the VA, and on and on had me being dead, and I can tell you it was so rewarding to let them know they were talking to Patrick McNeese, and yes, I could prove to them by coming to their office. In fact, I did have to go to Social Security and the VA to show them I was indeed alive. So in ending, if you read this book and don't have God in your life and still believe miracles only happened while Jesus Christ walked the earth, then my biggest hope is that after reading this book, you will have some type of enlightenment and believe without a doubt that miracles still occur today.

My main purpose in life when I got home was to tell at least one person a day my story so they could realize that miracles happen in today's world. What is totally amazing to me is that from the very first person I told, she told me of even more of a miracle that happened in her life, when both she and her baby lived when the doctors didn't give either of them any hope of living. And on and on people told me about miracles that had happened personally to them or to someone they knew. It's amazing that by the grace of God, my biography is now complete. And as you find from the very beginning, this book is mainly based on all the injuries, accidents, and operations that have occurred in the last sixty-seven years of my life.

I want it to be known that the most important thing I want people to take away if they read this book is that I'm not special in any sense of the word. There are so many people with so many more challenges in their lives than what I have had, and they continue to be part of the inspiration that led me to want to write this book from the beginning when I first started writing back in 2001, even before I was married.

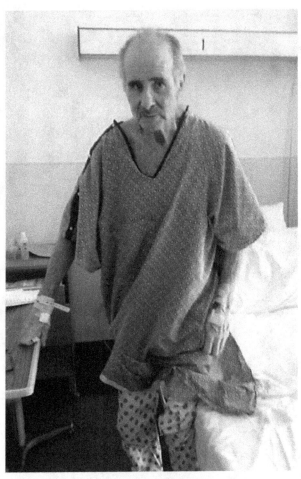

March 1 2019
Day I got out of hospital 123 lbs

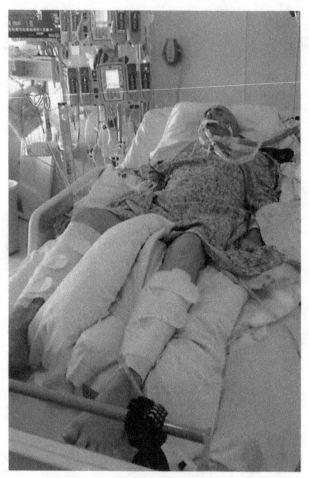

Life support
December 2018

1 week before hospital
December 2 2018
185-190 lbs

ABOUT THE AUTHOR

This is the first book that Patrick McNeese has written, and he began writing it in 2001. Since that time, he has changed the title many times; but because of his recent experiences, he decided to name it Miracle Man. Patrick is a native of California, having been born in Long Beach and being raised on a small island known as Lido Isle in the Newport Beach Harbor. He is the middle child of five siblings, having an elder sister, an elder brother, and two younger brothers. He went to Newport Elementary, a school on the Balboa Peninsula whose backyard and playground were the Pacific Ocean. He also went to and was confirmed at the Lady of Mount Carmel, a Catholic church that also was on the Balboa Peninsula. From an early age, Patrick's real passion was sports, and especially the one he seemed to excel at was baseball, and later in high school, it would be football. Although he was very small in high school to play football, it did not seem to bother him, because although legally blind and small, he tried to make up for it in toughness and never giving up. He went on to graduate from Newport Harbor High School and from there was in and out of colleges for the next four or five years, never to receive a degree. He always loved to write in school, including poetry, and his favorite subjects were English and history. He worked in construction, and unfortunately, he got injured while working and was put through school to receive a certificate as a computer analyst and computer programmer. He really did not like working on computers and was fortunate enough to find the profession he loved, by becoming a real estate appraiser. He currently resides in Huntington Beach, California, and is retired and still loves to write.